International and Co[r] Labour History

Socialist History 17

Rivers Oram Press
London, Sydney and New York

Editorial Team
Kevin Morgan
Stephen Woodhams
Willie Thompson
David Parker
Mike Waite
David Morgan
Heather Williams
Julie Johnson

Editorial Advisors
Noreen Branson
Rodney Hilton
Eric Hobsbawm
David Howell
Monty Johnstone
Victor Kiernan
David Marquand
Ben Pimlott
Pat Thane

All editorial enquiries to Kevin Morgan, Department of Government, University of Manchester M13 9PL or Kevin.Morgan@man.ac.uk

Published in 2000
by Rivers Oram Press, an imprint of Rivers Oram Publishers Ltd
144 Hemingford Road, London N1 1DE

Distributed in the USA by
New York University Press, 838 Broadway. New York, NY 10003–4183

Distributed in Australia and New Zealand by
UNIReps, University of New South Wales, Sydney, NSW 2052

Set in Garamond by
NJ Design Associates
and printed in Great Britain by
T.J. International Ltd, Padstow

This edition copyright © 2000 Socialist History Society
The articles are copyright © 2000 Stefan Berger, Paulo Fontes, David Grove, Karen Hunt, Paul Kelemen, Sheila Rowbotham

No part of this journal may be produced in any form, except for the quotation of brief passages in criticism, without the written permission of the publishers. The right of the contributors to be identified as the authors has been asserted by them in accordance with the Copyright, Designs and Patents Act 1988

British Library Cataloguing in Publication Data
A catalogue record for this publication is available from the British Library
ISBN 1 85489 118 0 (hb)
ISBN 1 85489 119 7 (pb)
ISSN 0969 4331

Contents

Guest Editorial   v
Stefan Berger

'Shush Mum's Writing'   1
Personal narratives by working-class women in the
early days of British women's history
Sheila Rowbotham

'The Immense Meaning of it All'   22
The challenges of internationalism for British socialist
women before the First World War
Karen Hunt

Labour's Africa and the Mau Mau Rebellion   43
Paul Kelemen

The 'Strike of 400,000' and the Organisation of   61
Workers in São Paulo, Brazil, 1957
Paulo Fontes

Design for Utopia?   76
David Grove

Reviews   82

South African communism
Dale T. McKinley, *The ANC and the Liberation Struggle.
A critical political biography* (Allison Drew)

Futures and pasts
Tim Jordan and Adam Lent (eds), *Storming the Millenium.
The new politics of change* (George McKay)

Organising the internet
Eric Lee, *The Labour Movement and the Internet* (Lee Salter)

International communisms
Tauno Saarela and Kimmo Rentola (eds), *Communism National and
International* (Francis King)

Chartist portraits
Stephen Roberts and Dorothy Thompson, *Images of Chartism*;
John K. Walton, *Chartism* (John Charlton)

Not only sex, drugs and rock 'n roll
Geoff Andrews, Richard Cockett, Alan Hooper and Michael Williams
(eds), *New Left, New Right and Beyond. Taking the sixties seriously*
(Stephen Brindle)

Cutlasses and earrings
Jo Stanley (ed.), *Bold in her Breeches. Women pirates across the ages*
(Jane Tinkler)

Organising the poor
John Charlton, '*It Went Just Like Tinder*'. *The mass movement and New
Unionism in Britain 1889* (Judy Cox)

Conspiracy on a world stage
Peter Gowan, *The Global Gamble. Washington's Faustian bid for world
domination* (A.C. Weaver)

Guest Editorial

Why is there not more international and comparative labour history? I'd suggest two major reasons: first, the legacy of the thorough nationalisation of historiography in the nineteenth century. The classical age of nationalism and nation-building saw historians focus their work very much on their own nation, real or imagined, and the institutionalised context of historical text production was equally firmly structured along national lines.[1] Second, comparative history is difficult. Comparative historians have to be very familiar with at least two social contexts, often they need to be bi- (or multi) lingual, and they have to be conceptually and theoretically aware to an even higher degree than ordinary historians. They cannot necessarily rely on information gathered for one national context. So, for example, it has been virtually impossible to compare national statistics because the methods of compiling those differed greatly from one national context to the other. Furthermore, comparative studies always have to consider that similar developments might have taken place in different national contexts at different times. Synchronic comparisons are therefore not always the best way of proceeding, and they often have to be complemented by diachronic comparisons. Overall, the formulation of a general framework in which the comparison can take place is as indispensable as it is demanding.[2]

Why should there be more international and comparative labour history? First, because the comparative method is conceptually a powerful tool to explain historical developments, and explanation surely is one of the key tasks of historians. Comparisons are capable of undermining causal explanations for developments which have been constructed in national frameworks. If the comparative historian can demonstrate that developments in two countries were similar, although they had different causes, or if they can show that developments were different, although the same preconditions were in place, then national historical explanations often have to be rethought.

Second, the comparative method makes us perceive differences between national developments more sharply and makes us aware of the many peculiarities which shaped our national histories. However, an overt concentration of comparative labour history on such differences has led to the formulation of a variety of theories of special paths (*Sonderwege*) which has ultimately ended in a cul-de-sac. If comparative history ends in an assertion that all nations are special, then this is hardly any more than trivial and may even serve the political purpose of underpinning national identities. In this variant, comparative history is continuing the project of nation-building which was so close to the hearts of nineteenth-century historians.[3]

Third, the comparative method may equally serve the purpose of highlighting similarities in the developments of different social contexts. Empirical historical studies of several diverse social/national contexts may validate general theories and allow the setting up of typologies in which similar case studies are summarised into different 'types'. Finally, the comparative method allows us to overcome the focus on national history and allows the historian but also the wider public who read history, to set their own experiences in the context of that of other nations. In this way, the powerful myths of specific national characters may be usefully undermined.[4] Comparative history is thus conceptually and politically a useful tool in the historian's workshop.

However, it has been a difficult tool to acquire. The workshop of the comparative historian needs to be located at the intersection of two different national/social contexts, and in the past there have not been many individuals for whom such preconditions existed. The internationalist orientation of the labour movement undoubtedly produced some early pioneers of comparative labour history. They often were people who had lived in a different society from the one they had grown up in for some considerable time. This experience led them to implicit or explicit comparison.[5] Similarly the internationalist orientation of the student protest movement, the New Left and the feminist movement of the late 1960s led to a new wave of interest in comparison. Yet perhaps the biggest boost to comparative history was the move towards Europeanisation after the end of the Second World War. The ever-increasing integration of Western European states in the context of the European Union produced unprecedented opportunities for scholarly exchanges and co-operation beyond national boundaries. The setting up of the European Science Foundation in 1974 is just one example among many which demonstrates the willingness to transcend national borders after the disastrous experiences made with nationalism in the first half of the twentieth century. The changed institutional context of historical text production also allowed comparative history to come to the fore, and it is hence not surprising that we witness an increasing number of comparative studies from the 1970s onwards. However, the European context, whilst it has opened important avenues, also carries the danger of focussing attention too much on Western Europe. Eurocentrism and Euro-history need to be overcome by attempts to widen the parameters of comparison to Eastern Europe and indeed to a world history perspective.

The concentration on national history not only marginalised comparative history in the past, it also made it difficult for labour history to get established in the academy. Hence comparative labour history can be regarded as doubly marginalised. Labour history could only be firmly established across Western Europe after 1945.[6] In Britain the Society for the Study of Labour History and, of course, the Communist Party Historians' Group were important institutional anchors for labour history as were journals such as *Past and Present* and *New Left Review*. Initially, the focus of much labour history was firmly on organisational and institutional history, and it was only in the 1970s that, under the influence of both History Workshop and the feminist movement, the emphasis shifted to the experiences, perceptions and subjectivities of individual historical actors, in particular ordinary workers and their everyday lives. Traditional labour movement history soon found itself in crisis, a crisis reinforced by the long-term decline of class as a social reality across Western Europe, the triumphalism of the political right in British politics throughout the 1980s, and the conceptual attacks on class by poststructuralism. Today there is broad agreement that labour history needs to get away from its narrow focus on organisational and institutional history if it wants to appeal to a new generation of students and scholars who have been, for some time now, voting with their feet and choosing different themes and topics. What we are witnessing is surely not the end of labour history,[7] but perhaps the end of labour history as we used to know it.

In the light of such general developments in the field of labour history, it must be rather worrying that most comparative labour history so far is strongly focussed on organisations, institutions and ideas. In particular the history of working-class parties and trade unions has been the focus of many a comparative study.[8] Certainly this has been the case, because much work on parties and unions had already been done in diverse national/social contexts. Nevertheless, one of the most urgent tasks of comparative labour history today is to extend its remit to the field of experiences and discourses.[9]

Here the article by Sheila Rowbotham can serve as an inspiration for comparative historians. Although she concentrates on British working-class women, the questions she develops in her article would be pertinent ones for comparative research: what were women's political perceptions in different social/national contexts? What alternative memories become available in female narratives about the past? The personal feelings and subjective sensibilities Rowbotham investigates reveal the complex gendering of class consciousness in the British context. Comparative research could sharpen our awareness of which factors contributed in which ways to the forms that such consciousness took in diverse social/national contexts.

If comparative labour history has to reach beyond organisation and ideology to experience and perception, it also cannot be carried out without taking into account the international dimension. National labour movements, just like national societies, did not develop in isolation from each other. Events which took place in one country often had important repercussions on developments in other countries. So, for example, Friedhelm Boll, investigating the European strike waves of 1889–90, found it impossible to analyse events in national isolation.[10] All European (and non-European?) states are hybrids, and have relied to a considerable degree on the cultural transfer of ideas, concepts and models in their specific national developments. Especially in the early days of socialism individuals played a crucial role as mediators between two or more different cultures and societies, facilitating such cultural transfer and allowing for the reception of ideas originally developed in different national and social contexts.

We encounter several of those remarkable individuals in the article of Karen Hunt. Internationalism and feminism were equally integral to both Dora Montefiore's and Margaret MacDonald's socialism. Both travelled extensively, had a wide network of comrades in diverse national contexts and were not shy to draw comparisons between different societies. Their 'women-focussed socialism', however, fitted badly with both the non-socialist women's groups and with the Socialist International.[11] Ultimately they were not fully accepted in either the socialist or the suffrage internationals. To make matters worse, they often used the international arena to prolong and continue the national rivalry which was fuelled by party political, ideological and—in the case of Montefiore and MacDonald—personal differences. Other women socialists, such as Isabel Ford and Ethel Snowden did not try so persistently to square their socialism with their feminism. Instead, they decided to prioritise their concern for female suffrage over their commitment to socialism. Karen Hunt's insightful analysis of the meaning of internationalism for diverse British socialist women before the First World War highlights the urgent need to make the question of cultural transfer a central one for comparative labour history.

Montefiore's internationalism, in particular her experiences in Australia, had made her an anti-imperialist and an anti-racist. That the British Labour Party found it far more difficult to free itself from notions of Empire is the highly convincing suggestion of Paul Kelemen's article on the attitudes of the British Labour Party towards Kenya between 1918 and the early 1960s. Not only the nation but also race and ethnicity played an important role for the identity of workers and labour movements across the globe.[12] Notions of benign forms of colonialism were always widespread in Labour Party circles but Kelemen's story is such a depressing one because the party's humanitarian progressive agenda of the 1920s, which included a commitment to structural socio-economic reform, deteriorated in the post-war era to one which was hardly distinctive from the Conservative Party. While mainstream Labour representatives rarely spoke the language of Social Darwinism, Labour's position was informed by widespread notions of African cultural backwardness. However, as Kelemen argues, it was largely the concern with developing Kenya's economic potential that led the party to drop its earlier demands for structural reforms. His article, like Rowbotham's, highlights the urgent need to compare the attitudes of working-class parties towards colonialism and imperialism. Much important work has been carried out in diverse national contexts, but to date there is too little comparative work.

Fontes's article, like that of Kelemen, is also focussed on an area of traditional labour history: strikes and industrial relations have been a key concern for national labour historiographies for decades, and there is already a considerable amount of comparative work.[13] However, much of that comparative work has been focussed on Europe and North America, and it is time to extend the comparative frame to countries of the developing world. Whether paradigms and historical methods developed for the industrialised nations are appropriate for developing nations has been the focus of some debate in the past.[14] Yet, beyond and above such controversies, it seems to me that Fontes succeeds in showing the way towards innovative qualitative methods for the comparative history of strikes. He not only challenges the notion that the Kubitschek years in Brazil were an 'oasis of social stability', he also highlights very effectively the importance of workers on the shopfloor for the success of the so-called 'Strike of 400,000'. Once more his article demonstrates the need to transcend comparative labour movement history and focus on the factory as perhaps the most important place, where workers formed occupational identities, developed forms of group solidarity in the work process and operated as economic and political actors in diverse contexts. Furthermore, Fontes also points to the vital links which existed between the location of the factory and the surrounding neighbourhood. There is hardly any comparative research which would take into account the relationship between those different life worlds: factory, neighbourhood, family and the organisational and political sphere.[15]

None of the four articles featured in this issue is strictly comparative, but all of them, in their different ways, point the way forward for comparative labour history. New themes and methods have been developed over the past decade or so which need to be explored urgently in a comparative way. Almost ten years ago Richard Price suggested that comparison was one way to revitalise British labour history and to free it from its pronounced insularity.[16] Today one finds dedicated comparative labour historians working in many British universities. Over the past decade more and more conferences have attempted to introduce a comparative dimension to the study of labour history. And the study of British working-class organisations and the British working class is increasingly put into its proper international context. Much of that comparative history, however, tends to focus on comparisons which can be researched within the constraints of a single language. If we just look at the previous issue of *Socialist History*, the work of Neville Kirk, David Howell and Sheila Rowbotham are superb examples of excellent comparative research on UK/US topics.[17] It should also be noted that collaborative history can sometimes overcome the constraints of both language and an intimate knowledge of another social context. Yet, before one gets too enthusiastic, my impression, from looking through the *Labour History Review*'s annual bibliographies and theses and dissertations listings for the 1990s, is that the comparative perspective still remains a marginal one. The regionalisation of British labour history is undoubtedly one of its main strengths, but I wonder whether it also leads to an undue interest in antiquarianism and a willingness to shut off one's own little corner of the world against an intrusion of the 'other'. Why is it otherwise that a conference on textile workers in Oldham is still more likely to attract crowds than a conference on international and comparative labour history? Of course, as John Foster's controversial study[18] demonstrates, a comparative approach can even be applied to Oldham, and the strong regional research on British Labour should definitely be encouraged to take on board comparisons of different British regions. Of course there are other major difficulties apart from antiquarianism and insularity: perhaps the biggest obstacle is the (declining!) willingness of British schoolchildren to learn foreign languages and the often dubious quality of language provision in British schools. At universities the firm distinction between British and European history never ceases to amuse our continental European colleagues who come to visit our institutions of higher education. If we do not start to integrate the British historical experience with that of other nations/societies (not necessarily only European ones) in our university courses and curricula, and if our education system does not provide incentives for learning foreign languages, then the prospects for comparative history generally, including labour history, remain dim. Much excellent work on British labour history, often comparative in nature, is done beyond Britain's borders, but how many British labour historians have the linguistic ability to access this research?

Stefan Berger

Notes

1. Stefan Berger, Mark Donovan and Kevin Passmore (eds), *Writing National Histories. Western Europe since 1800* (London, 1999).
2. For a good introduction to some of the problems involved in practising comparative (labour) history see John Breuilly, *Labour and Liberalism in Nineteenth-century Europe. Essays in comparative history* (Manchester, 1992), pp.1–25.
3. For a critique of the special paths in comparative labour history see Stefan Berger, 'European labour movements and the European working class in comparative perspective', in Stefan Berger and David Broughton (eds), *The Force of Labour. The Western European labour movement and the working class in the twentieth century* (Oxford, 1995), pp.245–61.
4. See already Peter Stearns, 'National character and European labor history', *Journal of Social History*, vol. 4 (1970/71), pp.95–124.
5. An early prominent example is Egon Wertheimer, *Portrait of the Labour Party* (London, 1929), which is implicitly comparative, although focussed on one country. In the English language see also, for example, G.D.H. Cole, *A History of Socialist Thought, 1789–1939*, 5 vols (London, 1956) and Julius Braunthal, *History of the International*, 2 vols (London, 1966 and 1967).
6. Stefan Berger, 'The rise and fall of "critical" historiography? Some reflections on the historiographical agenda of the left in Britain, France and Germany at the end of the twentieth century', *European Review of History*, vol. 3, no. 2 (1996), pp.213–32.
7. Out of the growing literature on 'crisis' compare Patrick Joyce, 'The end of social history?', *Social History*, vol. 20 (1995), p.76, who lambasted British labour history as 'almost moribund', and John Belchem, 'Reconstructing labour history', *Labour History Review*, no. 62 (1997), pp.318–23.
8. A by no means exhaustive list of English works in this vein would include Sheri Berman, *The Social Democratic Moment. Ideas and politics in the making of interwar Europe* (Cambridge, MA, 1998); Donald Sassoon, *One Hundred Years of Socialism. The West European left in the twentieth century* (London, 1996); Willie Thompson, *The Communist Movement Since 1945* (Oxford, 1998); Gerd-Rainer

Horn, *European Socialists Respond to Fascism. Ideology, Activism and Contingency in the 1930s* (Oxford, 1996); Gregory M. Luebbert, *Liberalism, Fascism or Social Democracy. Social classes and the political origins of regimes in inter-war Europe* (Oxford, 1991); John Schwarzmantel, *Socialism and the Idea of the Nation* (London, 1991). Stefan Berger, *The British Labour Party and the German Social Democrats 1900–1931. A comparative study* (Oxford, 1994) also falls into that category.

9. Some initial work has, of course, already been done. See, for example, Axel Körner, *Das Lied von einer anderen Welt. Kulturelle Praxis im französischen und deutschen Arbeitermilieu 1840–1890* (Frankfurt am Main, 1997); Mary Jo Maynes, *Taking the Hard Road. Life course in French and German workers' autobiographies in the era of industrialization* (Chapel Hill, 1995); Stefan Berger, 'In the fangs of social patriotism: the construction of nation and class in inter-war autobiographies of British and German Social Democrats', *Archiv für Sozialgeschichte*, vol. 40 (2000).

10. Friedhelm Boll, *Arbeitskämpfe und Gewerkschaften in Deutschland, England und Frankreich. Ihre Entwicklung vom 19. zum 20. Jahrhundert* (Bonn, 1992).

11. On the difficulties of combining feminism and socialism in diverse national contexts see Helmut Gruber and Pamela Graves, *Women and Socialism, Socialism and Women* (Oxford, 1998).

12. W. R. Garscha and C. Schindler (eds), *Labour Movement and National Identity* (Vienna, 1994); Stefan Berger and Angel Smith (eds), *Nationalism, Labour and Ethnicity* (Manchester, 1999).

13. See, for example, J. Cronin, 'Theories of Strikes: why can't they explain the British experience', *Journal of Social History*, vol. 12 (1978/79), pp.194–220; Charles Tilly (ed.), *Strikes, Wars and Revolutions in an International Perspective* (Cambridge, 1989); Dick Geary, 'Protest and strike: recent research on "collective action" in England, Germany and France', in Klaus Tenfelde (ed.), *Arbeiter und Arbeiterbewegung im Vergleich* (Munich, 1986), pp.363–88.

14. Specifically on Latin America see the exchange between Charles Bergquist, 'Latin American labor history in comparative perspective: notes on the insidiousness of cultural imperialism', *Labor* (Canada), vol.25 (1990), pp.189–98, and Jeremy Adelman, 'Against essentialism: Latin American labor history in comparative perspective. A critique of Bergquist', *Labor* (Canada), vol. 27 (1991), pp.175–84.

15. Thomas Welskopp, *Arbeit und Macht im Hüttenwerk. Arbeits- und industrielle Beziehungen in den deutschen und amerikanischen Eisen- und Stahlindustrie von der 1860er bis zu den 1930er Jahren* (Bonn, 1994) provides a model for any such comparative research.

16. Richard Price, 'The future of British labour history', *International Review of Social History*, vol.36 (1991), pp.249–60.

17. See also Sheila Rowbotham, *A Century of Women. The history of women in Britain and the United States* (New York, 1997); Neville Kirk, *Labour and Society in Britain and the United States 1780–1939*, 2 vols (Aldershot, 1994).

18. John Foster, *Class Struggle and the Industrial Revolution. Early industrial capitalism in three English towns* (London, 1977).

Socialist History Journal

The *Socialist History Journal* explores and assesses the past of the socialist movement and broader processes in relation to it, not only for the sake of historical understanding, but as an input and contribution to the movement's future development. The journal is not exclusive and welcomes argument and debate from all viewpoints.

Socialist History titles include:

A Bourgeois Revolution?
Socialist History 1 · 1993
0 7453 08058

What Was Communism? Pt 1
Socialist History 2 · 1993
0 7453 08066

What Was Communism? Pt 2
Socialist History 3 · 1993
0 7453 08074

The Labour Party Since 1945
Socialist History 4 · 1994
0 7453 08082

The Left and Culture
Socialist History 5 · 1994
0 7453 08090

The Personal and the Political
Socialist History 6 · 1994
0 7453 08104

Fighting the Good Fight?
Socialist History 7 · 1995
0 7453 10613

Historiography and the British Marxist Historians
Socialist History 8 · 1995
0 7453 08120

Labour Movements
Socialist History 9 · 1996
0 7453 08139

Revisions?
Socialist History 10 · 1996
0 7453 08147

The Cold War
Socialist History 11 · 1997
0 7453 12411

Nationalism and Communist Party History
Socialist History 12 · 1997
0 7453 12675

Imperialism and Internationalism
Socialist History 13 · 1998
1 85489 1073

The Future of History
Socialist History 14 · 1998
1 85489 109X

Visions of the Future
Socialist History 15 · 1999
1 85489 1154

America and the Left
Socialist History 16 · 1999
1 85489 1170

'Shush Mum's Writing'*
Personal narratives by working-class women in the early days of British women's history

Sheila Rowbotham

In her *Working Life of Women in the Seventeenth Century*, the Fabian socialist historian Alice Clark declared that her 'bias...consisted in a conviction that the conditions under which the obscure mass of women live and fulfill their duties as human beings, have a vital influence upon the human race, and that a little knowledge of what these conditions have actually been in the past will be of more value to the sociologist than many volumes of carefully elaborated theory.'[1]

Her pioneering work of women's history was first published in 1919. It was republished in 1968 by Frank Cass and Company just before the first women's liberation groups formed in Britain and a new generation took up the enquiry into 'the conditions under which the obscure mass of women live'. This preoccupation with the everyday lives of working-class women was a powerful impetus in the emergence of women's history in Britain. It was to result in a quarrying of earlier autobiographical works which had been relatively neglected and to inspire a range of personal narratives and historical studies which used oral interviews.

Why was it that young middle-class or socially mobile young working-class women whose outlook was radical, iconoclastic and thoroughly 'modern' were so fascinated by autobiographies and lives which were so different from their own? The mysteries of history are the attitudes and assumptions which are never explicitly explained because they were regarded as self-evident at the time. And this is particularly true of an era like the late 1960s and 1970s which has not yet been mulled over by scholars but has faded into a generation's memory.

Part of the explanation is undoubtedly that the impulse to comprehend and celebrate what was obscure and everyday was there within a wider radical culture before it influenced the emergence of women's history. It was evident for example in kitchen-sink drama, in films, in literature and in the folk clubs which were part of the Campaign for Nuclear Disarmament from the late 1950s. There was both a quest to capture 'real experience' and a desire to record activities and ways of life which were vanishing. The raw and authentic were given a new respect, which sometimes involved a dismissal of more abstract theorising which was associated with privilege.

A sustained challenge to history as the story of the powerful was also appearing in several quarters. Oral history was pioneered not in the academy but by George Ewart Evans on the radio in the 1950s, while during the late 1950s and early 1960s Charles Parker's famous radio ballads combined Ewan McColl and Peggy Seeger's music with the documentary form. Programmes such as 'The Ballad of John Axon' and 'The Big Hewer' were to become classics of broadcasting.[2] Moreover by the mid-1960s works like E.P. Thompson's *The Making of the English Working Class* and the new historiography of the crowd in the French Revolution had created a new kind of a social history 'from below'. Instead of posing experience against theory, this was demonstrating how ideas developed *amidst* experience. History Workshop started by Raphael Samuel in 1968 at Ruskin, the trade union college in Oxford, became a gathering place for radical historians in which professors took the platform with worker students who documented their own lives and neighbourhoods. The first women's liberation conference in 1970 had its origins in a Ruskin History Workshop.

Other influences were evident in the emphasis on imagination and personal desire which accompanied the radicalisation of students and other young people after the May Events in Paris during 1968. Early feminist meetings could draw on a new left influenced by anti-colonial theory and the black movement in the United States in which the 'personal' had become part of the terrain of politics. The radical intellectual politics of the late 1960s were thus concerned about power not simply in politics or the economy but in the constitution and hold of knowledge. Domination could be manifest in the process of definition; it permeated personal relations and was embedded in language. These new perceptions about the scope of politics contributed to an assertion of subjectivity. Understanding based on experience was seen as a means of challenging the closed circuits of what was recognised as 'known'.

There were other less conscious influences at work too. The generation of young women who became active in women's liberation consciousness-raising groups had grown up amidst the popular culture of the 1950s. We read *True Confessions* and listened to the 'girl talk' groups long before we discovered Sartre. Songs like 'Will you still love me tomorrow?' were breaking the codes of what could be said. Nell Dunn's book of interviews, *Talking to Women* (1967) appeared just before the women's liberation consciousness-raising groups emerged in Britain. It expressed feelings about sexuality which were spoken among friends but which were not part of written culture.

Rediscovering memories

The first generation of young women to enter higher education in such numbers in Britain were in a terra incognita. In a collection of memories of the 1950s by feminists, *Truth, Dare or Promise*, Liz Heron observes: 'Many of us writing here express a sense of not belonging, of feeling like outsiders.'[3] Indeed, because our social and geographical mobility was unprecedented we were making up being women as we went along. Consequently we were open to experiment while listening for echoes; situating ourselves by making tangible what we had left. One way of seeking our bearings was to be through the testimonies of women who were like adopted grandmothers. The late 1960s was also a time when working-class women were stirring; more and more married women had been coming into the labour force and equal pay at last seemed a possibility. This new confidence among working women was an added impetus for the young intelligentsia to document and to learn from a source outside the academy.

A combination of social, political and economic factors thus converged to create a mood of cultural receptivity; a crucial starting point for any challenge to the dominant set of values. This was sustained by the emergence of the women's liberation movement which meant a whole series of urgent questions about the past were being persistently raised. This was to create a modest market for women's history outside academia from the early 1970s and later contribute to the growth of women's studies first in adult education and then in higher education and schools.

One of the initial areas of investigation and reinterpretation for the little group of feminist historians was the suffrage movement. Though this was still commonly presented as a hysterical paroxysm of upper-class women, it was nonetheless the political movement of women that we all knew about. The discovery of Hannah Mitchell's autobiography *The Hard Way Up* was revelatory for me. It had been published in 1968 and was quickly remaindered—I bought a copy while I was writing *Hidden from History* in the early 1970s. It describes the participation of a socialist shop worker from the North in the suffrage movement and shows how the vote for her and for other working-class local activists was inseparable from broader social reform. It also shows the interweaving of trade union, suffrage and socialist history which organisational histories documented as separate stories. Most fascinating was the glimpse into the interior world of politics. She records her resentment of Emmeline and Christabel Pankhurst's disregard for personal difficulties which made her feel used, yet was all too aware that the socialists often supported women with words not deeds. She remarked after she married a socialist:

> Even my Sunday leisure was gone for I soon found that a lot of the Socialist talk about freedom was only talk and these Socialist young men expected Sunday dinners and huge teas with home-made cakes, potted meat and pies exactly like their reactionary fellows.[4]

This was a novel take on labour history which contained little on personal attitudes and the sexual division of labour. It also provided evidence of a lost political strand. Local activists can surface in one movement and then vanish from view but Hannah Mitchell's autobiographical account makes it possible to follow through the impetus of her feminism and socialism in the changing context of the 1920s and 1930s. *The Hard Way Up* documents a labour feminism between the wars in her local government work, pointing out the needs of women and children in municipal parks, campaigning for public wash houses, questioning the hierarchies in hospitals, as well as fighting for unemployed women and the right of married women to work. These were all causes which were to become more difficult during the depression. Hannah Mitchell also noted a strong current of anti-feminism in the Labour Party, which labour men were inclined to dress up with 'admirable sentiments about the domestic hearth, with "mother's influence" as a tear jerker' or go 'all Marxian', stressing 'the bad economics of two incomes going into one home, while men with a capital "M" were unemployed'.[5]

The story of the manuscript is itself an indication of how particular political perceptions can be eclipsed until attitudes shift. It shows how the lives and aspirations of women like Hannah Mitchell are by no means automatically received into the annals of history. Her son Geoffrey Mitchell, who edited the original manuscript, describes its chequered career before it got into print:

> Hannah Mitchell worked on it in the last years of the Second World War and in the years immediately after it. She was secretive about the task and must have spent hours at work at her typewriter while her husband was out; indeed she must have taken great care to put her papers away when anyone was around, for she kept her friends and her family in the dark until the whole was completed.
>
> The fate of the manuscript is also not without interest, for although

she was not unpushing in trying to get a publisher to accept it, at the time none found it interesting enough to undertake. During her lifetime she had to be content to see short extracts published in interested journals and to accept praise and admiration from a few friends to whom she sent the work.

Undoubtedly she was disappointed and frustrated in this, for the manuscript was put away and only recovered among her papers at her death in 1956.[6]

A personal encounter in the early 1970s gave me another insight into the connections between suffrage and the labour movement. When I was teaching in the Workers' Educational Association in Stanmore, West London, a woman in my class introduced me to a former constitutional suffragist and Independent Labour Party member who had also been active in the shop workers' union, Florence Exten-Hann. She was in her eighties when I met her and unable to get about much. She was nonetheless keen to help the new women's movement, but she had read in the press how we were mainly preoccupied with bra burning. 'Of course,' she said a little sadly, 'You're not interested in the trade unions like we were.' We stared at each other across the gap of sixty years. For the version of suffrage history which had been transmitted to my generation had similarly obscured links between feminism and class politics. The account Florence gave me of her life, which was published in the socialist feminist magazine *Red Rag*, showed an overlapping involvement in suffrage, trade unionism, socialism and the peace movement.[7]

Another working-class socialist suffrage campaigner, Jessie Stephen, did participate in the Bristol women's liberation group and in an interview with Gloden Dallas and Suzie Fleming in *Spare Rib* magazine reflected on the vagaries of the historical record. 'Truly you need seven-league boots to keep up with an untruth.'[8]

The initial openings for reinterpreting labour and feminist history were in feminist and alternative radical journals and papers, which were of course themselves ephemeral. However, the emergence of the women's movement was to have an impact on existing publishers and contribute to the creation of several new feminist presses. Of these, Virago was to play a particularly important role during the 1970s and early 1980s in making works documenting the lives of working-class women available. One of the founders of Virago, Ursula Owen, who had previously worked at Frank Cass, was personally interested in women's and labour history.

The new questions about the past stimulated by the women's movement were to uncover a lost trail of working-class women's activism. The Lancashire links between trade unionism, socialism and feminism were explored in depth when Jill Norris and Jill Liddington produced *One Hand Tied Behind Us* about the radical suffragists in 1978. Jill Liddington followed this with a biography of the northern working-class campaigner for socialism and for women, Selina Cooper, in 1984 and Anna Davin did an introduction to the collected writings of another Lancashire socialist suffragist, Ada Nield Chew. This rediscovery of the radical suffragists relied on written sources but also on the testimonies of daughters.

An alternative memory transmitted through generations was thus one of the sources for the contested and forgotten legacy of women's contribution to the public world of labour politics. Jill Liddington commented in her article *Looking for Mrs Cooper* that ingenuity in detection was necessary, because the obvious records were invariably not there:

> While male labour historians could rely on the *From Workbench to Westminster* genre of autobiographies, feminist historians have no *Washtub to Westminster* equivalents.[9]

The awakened interest in the political involvement of working-class women was accompanied by curiosity about the everyday lives of women. Virago reprinted the early twentieth century study of poverty by Maud Pember Reeves, *Round About A Pound A Week* in 1979 with an introduction by Sally Alexander. In 1983 they did Clementina Black's survey *Married Women's Work*, first published in 1915. Oral interviews provided a direct route to more contemporary everyday lives. They were a vital source for reflections on domestic and personal relationships which feminist historians were seeking to validate. Mary Chamberlain's *Fenwomen: A Portrait of Women in an English Village* (Virago, 1975) was an early and notable example. In looking at rural women she was following in a tradition set by George Ewart Evans and Ronald Blythe's popular work *Akenfield: A Portrait of an English Village* (1969), but focusing explicitly on women. When Jean McCrindle and I collected the interviews for *Dutiful Daughters* (1977) we were interested in covering the whole span of personal life and public action. We did not situate the book in one community, aiming to include a range of women geographically. We were trying not simply to document experience but to counter the cultural marginalisation of working-class women's reflections on their lives. Aware that older working-class women rarely featured even in women's liberation magazines and papers, we consciously weighted the selection towards them. We also recorded Barbara Marsh who had come from Jamaica to Britain in the early 1960s. We saw the collection as an extension in another form of the consciousness-raising group. While each individual story was of interest the impact of the combination of testimonies became something more. In the introduction we explained:

> We wanted to show through the interviews that if the experience of most women is regarded as unworthy of recording it is not because it is in itself uninteresting, meaningless or trivial, but because of the criteria which are normally brought to bear when the decision to record is taken.[10]

This feminist challenge to cultural exclusion coincided with a creative phase in community publishing, made possible by the new technology of offset litho, but inspired by radical community politics. Local groups began chronicling working-class people's memories both through interviews and by encouraging writers. The Worker Writers' Federation was formed in 1976, providing a national link to disparate initiatives.[11] The community bookshop Centerprise in Hackney played a pioneering role and a Workers' Education Association class set out to build up a collective history through a project called 'The People's Autobiography of Hackney' in 1976.

These grassroots chronicles were not feminist inspired, though they documented women's wrongs and shared a common commitment to resisting cultural exclusion. However, because they included women as well as men they were to provide a source for women's history. There was, *When I Was a Child* by Dot Starn from Hackney, and from Queenspark in Brighton came Daisy Noakes' *The Town Beehive. A Young Girls' Lot in Brighton 1910–1934*. This sold out and was reissued in 1980 with her sequel about her marriage to an agricultural labourer, *Faded Rainbow: Our Married Years*. In 1979 Strong Words from Durham produced a pamphlet called *But The World Goes On The Same. Changing times in Durham pit villages*. The group put together writings, interviews and poems by miners, textile workers, shop assistants, schoolchildren and housewives.

These pamphlets broke down the customary boundaries between the spoken and the written word. The project of the collective autobiography told the history of specific experiences of class in particular localities. They followed in the tradition established by social historians such as E.P. Thompson in presenting an understanding of class which spanned work and community. They also added personal comments about childhood or sexuality which provided insights for the new focus on culture and popular attitudes emerging within both women's history and within social history.

They are not dry or ponderous records; they express a sense of power in claiming space which had been denied and celebrate the confidence developed in the 1960s and 1970s when things did seem to be improving for many working-class people. In retrospect, the explosion of community publishing during the 1970s and early 1980s can be seen as an historical document not only in the past that was directly recounted, but in the indirect expression of a more recent mood of assurance about entitlement which was beginning to affect how working-class women, as well as men, looked back on their own lives.

Radio and television were popularising autobiographical accounts in the same period. The late 1960s and early 1970s saw the publication of several paperbacks written in a breezy style laced with home truths. For instance Margaret Powell's descriptions of domestic service and her married life, *Below Stairs* and *The Treasure Upstairs* were published by Pan. She was humorous and down to earth:

> I did sometimes wonder after struggling all those years to get married what all the fuss was about....Mind you I wasn't any Lady Chatterley and Albert wasn't the gamekeeper.[12]

Other examples in a similar vein are Grace Foakes' *My Part of the River* (first published in 1972 and issued in paperback by Futura in 1976) and Dorothy Scannell, *Mother Knew Best* (Macmillan 1974 and Pan 1977), both about East London.

The existence of a mainstream popular readership provided an outlet for working-class women's reminiscences way beyond feminist or community publishing. It is as if some intimation of the enormous changes occurring in society was being expressed in an appetite for stories of a way of life which was fast vanishing. The more popular autobiographies communicated grit and resolution amidst hardship, a spirit of community and human warmth where everyone pulled together. They thus conserved a version of the good old days, despite poverty but they also marked a democratic recognition of the contribution of women who would have been hidden from history. There were to be conservative echoes in the explosion of patriotic sentiment around the Queen's Jubilee in 1977 and then later when Margaret Thatcher became Prime Minister in the Falklands/ Malvinas War. More radical echoes were the expanding community adult education projects attended by working-class women and the poems, stories and songs women produced during the miners' strike of 1984–5.

While the purposes of seeking out working-class women's memories differed they shared a common feature; the individual life story became public through channels of significance in which the women gained an audience as representatives of an obscured and subordinated culture. This was an advance because it enlarged the terrain of what could be heard; it enabled suppressed voices to find listeners. It did however also mean a certain containment, for it restrained the deeper probing possible when you are not organising memory to prove an explicit point. This was a freedom which remained with the privileged.

Virginia Woolf had recognised this dilemma in her perceptive essay on class and gender written as an introduction to the collection of life stories by members of the Women's Cooperative Guild, published by the Hogarth Press in 1931, *Life As We Have Known It*. Because she had not known a life similar to theirs she could accentuate the difference:

> They touched nothing lightly. They gripped papers and pencils as if they were brooms. Their faces were firm and heavily folded and lined with deep lines. It seemed as if their muscles were always taut and on the stretch. Their eyes looked as if they were always set on something actual—on saucepans that were boiling over, on children who were getting into mischief. Their lips never expressed the lighter and detached emotions that come into play when the mind is perfectly at ease about the present. No, they were not in the least detached and easy and cosmopolitan. They were indigenous and rooted to one spot.[13]

When Margaret Llewelyn Davies, the middle-class founder of the Women's Cooperative Guild, gave her literary friend the faded bundle of letters which were to turn into *Life As We Have Known It*, she said nervously that she hoped they would mean that 'the women would cease to be symbols and become individuals'.[14] But the pathway through to cultural hegemony is not straightforward and the journey into history is beset by concealed and unexpected snares. Virginia Woolf discerned an inequality which became visible even as the women told their life stories. They came forward to lay their claim to be part of history as representatives of the dignity of their class and sex, yet this presentation of individual identity as part of a wider social meaning also restricted imagination, fancy and speculation. It is after all the mark of privilege to simply assume to 'be' in the world, without any more ado or looking over your shoulder to see what anyone thinks of you.

This is true not only of the story but of the telling. Consciousness of subordination influences what is told and the organisation of what is remembered as significant. It can also make for self-consciousness about familiar ways of expressing experience. It was still all too apparent forty years after *Life As We Have Known It* was first published. For example, when I interviewed a friend and former neighbour, Barbara Marsh from Jamaica, for *Dutiful Daughters*, during the early 1970s, she expressed concern because the rhythms of her speech were not grammatical like written English. She was worried that this could confirm the prejudices of white readers about West Indians, a realistic wariness about the power to give her account a hostile and judgmental meaning. The dominance within language was moreover accompanied by clashes in values about sexuality and family:

> For instance look now, our system back home is different from here. Honestly but it is a silly system over here and a selfish and mean system. They cut off all communication, and then—you see, that's the English system where you are taught to suppress everything. Hide things like skeletons in the cupboard. That's not necessary.[15]

One consequence of the material which surfaced as a result of curiosity about 'real' experience was a recognition of the complexities and nuances of differing realities. However if brushing culture against the grain was to reveal unsuspected snags, it has also opened up a rich source for thinking about women's political grassroots activism, about work and domestic life and about sexuality and aspiration. All these broaden the terms of reference of the old question 'What do women want?' which in turn extends how the scope of politics can be defined and how a gendered class-consciousness can be considered.

Hardship and personal perceptions

The very tightness of circumstance which Virginia Woolf had noted means that a tension between acceptance and resistance is frequently evident. For example Daisy Foakes wrote in *My Part of the River*, 'People of that era knew how to make the best of every situation',[16] but she could also cast an acerbic eye on the public rituals of class union. On Empire Day she waved her flag and sang 'Deeds of Glory' but she still *wondered*.

We sang and believed we were the mightiest nation on earth. But how many I wonder felt as I did. While all this went on I'm afraid I sang with my mouth only, not from the heart. For I saw only the same high walls and thought to myself 'we sing of our possessions while not one of us here owns as much as a flowerpotful of earth.'[17]

In *Our Common History*, Paul Thompson's oral history collection which was influenced by both feminist history and community publishing, the Italian feminist historian Luisa Passerini theorised this collision between defiance and submission in the differing context of responses of Italian working-class people to fascism. She argued for approaching consciousness as 'problematic potentiality, never guaranteed yet nevertheless possible'.[18] She added, 'Here is the clue to the ambivalence of "needs" which always combine both a reference to the full potential in human nature and, on the other hand, a partial acceptance of the existing order which denies their realisation.'[19]

This is graphically expressed in Dot Starn's account of the restricted options of work for a working-class girl early in the century. She tells how she went for her first job to a florist called Miss Craven, who announced: 'I don't pay wages you know. Many people would pay me to teach them the trade.'[20] One day an old lady gave Dot a sixpenny piece for delivering flowers. The memory hurt sixty years later:

> Old Mother Craven said: 'Did they give you anything?'
> 'Yes.'
> 'That is not for you that is mine.'
> When I told my mother she said: 'She had no right to take that money away from you.' But that was as far as it went. Mum was so proud and I was only young. I would not allow anyone to do a thing like that to a child of mine.[21]

The authority of a parent could not prevail in the world of work. But Dot was beginning to find her feet:

> One day I said:
> 'May I go to the ladies please?'
> 'Are you sure you must? I can't keep giving you pennies.' I had never asked before. I left a few days after and got a job in Clerkenwell fixing crowns on the tops of hollow needles that were used by dentists to freeze gums.[22]

The narrow scope of realisable needs comes through again and again, even in the post-Second World War era. In an oral interview in *But The World Goes On The Same*, for instance, Elizabeth Harris, who went to work in a clothing factory near Durham when she came from India, describes how all the factory women stared at her because 'I was the only coloured girl in the town then'.[23] She remarks on the part-time work they were doing,

> Most of the women were driven out to work because they needed money to keep the house going and for their children. Many of us wouldn't be

working if we had enough money. There was a saying that if you worked in the factory that you were either among the needy or the greedy. Most of us were needy. For the women with families, work was possible because of the part-time system. At one time one of the managers tried to move everyone on to a full-time basis but then who was going to look after the children, taking and collecting them from school. We wouldn't have any of it, so the management never got it through. I only moved to full-time when my husband became disabled. Most were like me, we were working out of necessity.[24]

The tight boundaries of necessity also encompassed the time and energy expended in the home. In the early years of this century housework was physically arduous and washing really took a day. Merlin Clarke, one of my students in a Workers' Education Association class in the 1970s, interviewed her mother-in-law for an essay. The account was published in the *Spare Rib Reader* and includes a graphic description of the laborious rituals of her wash day:

Once you had your fuel, you had to fill your copper by hand and when the water was hot you ladled it out into a tin bath when you would use a rubbing board and blocks of soap. Once all the washing had been rubbed it went back into the refilled copper together with bleaching soda and ordinary soda and would be left to boil for twenty minutes. It was a steamy job, pushing it down every so often with a copper stick.[25]

After the children grew older and went out to work a little more money came into the household. Hudson's Soap Powder could be substituted for the two kinds of soda. Merlin Clarke recorded:

When the wash had finished boiling it would be 'blued' with a Reckitt's blue bag or starched and finally it would be wrung out through a hand operated mangle. After the wash had been dried it would be ironed on the kitchen table on an old piece of blanket with a sheet or piece of cotton over that. The irons would be hot irons heated by the fire and the only sure way to see if they were hot enough would be to spit on them.[26]

Such precise and detailed descriptions of the outer circumstances of existence convey how much energy had to be concentrated on daily life. Acquiescence to the demands of this relentless necessity was the only means of continuing. Consequently the expression of emotion frequently comes only through tiny chinks and cracks. For instance after another description of washing day, Grace Foakes writes:

> On each packet of 'Sunlight' soap there were the words, ' Why does a woman look older than a man?' It went on to explain the merits of the soap, but it was small wonder that women *did* look old at forty.[27]

The most extreme experiences are frequently conveyed with an economy of expression which testifies to that hidden form of class inequality in which the tragedies of the poor are chronicled only as statistics and the dead are despatched impersonally. This was to persist after 1945, despite the benefits of the post war National Health Service. Daisy Noakes describes how she looked after her invalid husband, a former agricultural worker, until it became too much:

> When the nurse called one morning, I could not stop my tears they had been flowing since the previous day. I was not crying, yet the tears would not stop.[28]

The doctor suggested that her husband should go to hospital for five weeks:

> Five weeks it was to the day when I had a phone call from the hospital to say George had passed away an hour previously.[29]

Rebellion against accepting the confines of necessitous existence made Kathleen Woodward, the author of the autobiographical novel *Jipping Street*, fight her way out of the class and gender destiny set by her upbringing in early-twentieth-century London. Her story shows how a degree of social mobility opened up first through feminist and socialist networks and then through writing. It was probably the severity of her mother which gave her the toughness to scramble out, but it left a harsh memory:

> She sweated and laboured for her children…without stint or thought, but was utterly oblivious to any need we might cherish for sympathy in our little sorrows, support in our strivings. She simply was not aware of anything beyond the needs of our bodies.[30]

Sometimes, exhaustion exploded into rage:

> when she touched that extreme verge of tiredness in mind and body and

would not give way it seemed to revenge itself and become a fierce anger....

She had no love to give us, and, thank God she never pretended what she did not feel; but children miss the presence of love and wilt, when they are not embittered, in its absence.

At home it was always wintry.[31]

While some women such as Grace Foakes recollected their mothers as gentle stoical martyrs, bitter memories like Kathleen Woodward's are extremely common among women who were children before the Second World War. 'I hate my mother' said Maggie Fuller, the Scottish wife of an agricultural labourer in the Scottish Lowlands, when Jean McCrindle and I interviewed her for *Dutiful Daughters*.[32] There is nothing particularly mysterious about the resentment. Working-class mothers assumed that girls should do what they had to do. Hard pressed by overwork and repeated childbearing, disliking farm life in the Derbyshire hills, Hannah Mitchell's mother flew into wild rages and worked the children mercilessly, especially the girls:

She made us sweep and scrub, turn the heavy mangle on washing days and the still heavier churn on butter-making days. Stone floors had to be whitened, brasses and steel fire-irons polished every week. On winter evenings there was sewing by hand, making and mending shirts and underwear. At eight years old my weekly task was to darn all the stockings for the household, and I think my first reactions to feminism began at this time when I was forced to darn my brothers' stockings while they read or played cards or dominoes.[33]

Robert Roberts, remembering life in Salford in *The Classic Slum* (1971), thought he could detect a new spirit of independence after the First World War and Sally Alexander noted new ways of becoming a woman among the London working class from the 1920s. Not only material circumstances but 'aspirations' were changing.[34] Nevertheless, incomprehension between mothers and daughters could remain. That this was not a static relationship however is illustrated by Jean Mormont, a London night cleaner. In *Dutiful Daughters* she reflected on her perception of her mother as a young girl in the 1930s in the light of her own understanding as a mother of a large family in the 1970s:

Sitting looking out the window, that's the memory I've got of my mum...But I think I understand more now myself, because I think after having a few children like that—I mean she had a hell of a lot (18) and I've only had seven, but it does take all the life out of you, this is true. I mean you don't realise it till you get older. I mean I know how I feel myself sometimes....she must have been ill in herself, she just couldn't do it. Because I know I get me good days and I get me bad days like, but I can still nip around, but it does pull you down, it's true, it does. I can never remember my mother looking young.[35]

Though the working class in the first half of the century was much surveyed, personal feelings were rarely documented—subjective sensibility was something that belonged in Bloomsbury. Personal narratives begin to correct the imbalance. These accounts of family relations also question the comfortable assumption that there was ever an era of pristine family values which were mutually accepted. Instead, working-class women bore a heavy burden of toil and their relations with their daughters could often suffer as a consequence.

They question sexual stereotypes too, breaking through external definitions of class and gender to reveal distinctive differences which can be blurred in broad sociological sweeps. Jean Mormont's father, for instance, was a harsh man, as was Grace Foakes', but Hannah Mitchell's in an earlier generation was gentle and kind though unable to stand up to her mother's rages. One of the younger women in *Dutiful Daughters*, Linda Peffer, felt cultural attitudes about working-class men and women were completely at variance with her actual family. Her father was the sensitive one, in contrast to her fierce and forceful mother. Growing up in North London in the 1950s she used to wish that her family fitted the conventions:

when you're a child you like your family to be like everybody else's don't you? You know Sunday dinner and the women being mum...I suppose we were what would be classed as a typical working-class family. If it ever exists!...the difference is that a lot of people lead a sort of cover-up, charade...I think my mum didn't cover up, because she wanted to be herself, and then I think because of all the pressures of society she must have got very guilty about it, and so there must have been this terrible sort of mixture going on...[36]

Discomfort with the accepted forms of femininity is usually regarded as middle-class angst, remote from working-class women in the 1950s.

All that carry on

Working-class women before the Second World War were similarly assumed not to have sexual feelings or thoughts on desire. It was still hard for middle-class women to discuss sexuality in public during the 1930s. The older women in *Dutiful Daughters*, from the vantage point of the 1970s, did however want to talk about sexuality. Their accounts reveal how frequently it was surrounded by fear, revulsion, ignorance, anxiety and suffering; their comments provide an indication of the sensual denial obscured in the current nostalgia for 'traditional' family values.

The Scots countrywoman, Maggie Fuller, observed:

> I'd rather do without it, it's been left like that you know what I mean….as regards sex it's no use—if I hadn't been a kind of stable person I am sure I'd have gone off my ruddy head. You know I'd rather not have it, all that carry on, you know. It's maybe me that's cold, I don't know, I've never talked about it—too late in life to talk about it now.[37]

The idea that you were either intellectual or sexy died hard. Annie Davison, active in the Independent Labour Party in Glasgow after the First World War and a member of the socialist theatre group the Clarion Players, describes herself as the serious type:

> I was always considered a bit prudish among the Clarion Players drama group. Those I got I could immediately sense were playboys—well, I had no time for them, and I think also because I was rather a plain person myself. Not a sexy type of person. I was more inclined to be intellectual than sexy.[38]

An obvious restraint was that reliable contraception was not easily available. Annie Williams who went to London as a nurse and later a nanny in the 1920s was in the sexual vanguard; she spent a couple of nights with Douglas, her husband-to-be, before they married and she then went to Marie Stopes' birth-control clinic and was fitted with a diaphragm. Young married women by whatever means between the wars were reducing the number of children by birth control, though only a minority had diaphragms. In *Dutiful Daughters* Annie Williams looked back from the perspective of the permissive 1960s and 1970s:

> I didn't feel guilty about it…I haven't got any inhibitions about it at all—

> but I have never had an orgasm, you know. I've nearly got there sometimes, but I've never actually had one and I can't discuss it with Douglas. He thinks that it is a lot of things that are out of Womens Lib and all that.[39]

The cultural restrictions on discussion of sexuality were accentuated by a lack of time and space for pleasure and exploration. The day after Daisy Noakes was married her husband had to be back at work: 'No honeymoon period for us. The gentry could not allow such luxuries. It was like getting blood out of a stone to get a day to marry.'[40]

Jessie Stephen, who went on from campaigning for the suffrage to activity in the Workers' Birth Control Group in the 1920s, made a rare allusion to lesbianism in the interview she gave to Gloden Dallas and Suzie Fleming in *Spare Rib* telling a story about a man heckling her in Sheffield with: '"Would you rather sleep with a woman or a man?" I said "A woman wouldn't you?" There was a burst of laughter at this and he silently stole away.'[41]

She added:

> Some of the women lived together but of course the ordinary working girls never got to that stage. They hadn't got the philosophy to start with and they couldn't have afforded to live like that. It's still true. There isn't the money there. They might be prepared to experiment if they had the means. There was also a cult of free love in the socialist movement in my youth but we won't go into that too deeply.[42]

Annie Davison and her husband did consider a free union, but they rejected the idea because the consequences for the women and children were often so severe. While the sexual responses of working-class women varied individually, material circumstances such as contraception, time and income combined with prevailing cultural attitudes in the first three decades of the twentieth century to keep the possibilities for self-conscious choice extremely narrow. Delight seemed to be enmeshed with retribution. In *Jipping Street*, Lil who danced and sang and flirted, died in childbirth aged twenty. Her death marked the end of dreams of an 'impossible future'.[43]

If it was hard to describe pleasure it was equally difficult for a member of the Women's Cooperative Guild to tell of sexual coercion. The following stiff account of violation appears in *Life As We Have Known It*:

> When I was a girl of seventeen, my then employer, a gentleman of good position and high standing in the town, sent me to his home one night,

ostensibly to take a parcel of books but really with a very different object. When I arrived at the house all the family were away, and before he would allow me to leave he forced me to yield to him. At eighteen I was a mother.[44]

Grace Foakes says that the East London women had to put up with beatings from drunken husbands: 'The following day she would emerge with black eyes and swollen face, yet would not utter a word against her husband—and woe betide anyone who did.'[45] Vera Alsop, who was born in 1915, says in her interview in *But The World Goes On The Same* that in her mother's and grandmother's day in the Durham area,

> the man was the boss. He was the boss of the house, and if he wasn't the boss of the house he wasn't considered to be a man. Some bashing went on…The woman was supposed to sit there with a little black shawl on and wait for him coming in, and that's what most women did.[46]

Submission however was not the whole story. There were troublemakers who found ways of challenging what was 'supposed' and Vera's mother-in-law was one of them. She fought her husband back:

> He'd say 'You're supposed to be in at such and such a time.' and if she wasn't in by that time he used to lock her out. She was late getting home this one night and she got one of the lasses to let her in. She goes into the sitting room which was in darkness. Well, he heard her and ran in after her saying what he was going to do to her. And he was a big man. Anyway she got up on a chair and she took this tray of toffee (she used to make toffee to give to the bairns). My father-in-law had a baldy head and everytime he walked past her she hit him on the top of the head with the toffee. There was toffee all over the sitting room. Another time he came in drunk and started acting up so she got these rolls of paper. Hit him over the head with the rolls of paper. The next morning he couldn't remember. 'Bye. I don't know what's happened to me but my head's sore'. She says 'Will you look at all that paper. That got broke over your head last night.'[47]

With political hindsight Vera Alsop observed, 'This is what women's lib is all about you see. I don't go as far as they go perhaps but it's nice to know you have some rights. Because in those days you had no rights at all.'[48]

Like several of the other women interviewed in the 1970s she looks back at the first half of the century in the light of attitudes which had appeared in later decades. With the passing of time these testimonies tell us not simply about everyday life in the first part of the century, they indicate how the radicalism of the 1960s and 1970s reached some unexpected places. The impulse to document a wider human experience which took young middle-class feminists or community activists to working-class homes, could meet reciprocal questioning. When I interviewed a Leeds socialist clothing worker, Gertie Roche, in 1974 she asked me: 'Are you liberated in your own life?' Her query took me by surprise and put the interviewer's boot on the other foot.

The desire to express

The personal narratives themselves are full of surprises too. They challenge easy stereotypes and indicate the complexity of gendered class-consciousness. Our search for 'real' experience in the late 1960s and 1970s demonstrated just how varied and elusive this could be, a salutary lesson which made the next wave of oral history more theoretically self-conscious about what was being suppressed in remembering and how the recorder affects the narrative. But when all is said and done we were still correcting a great partiality—and one that has reasserted itself—the weighting of the record to the privileged and the powerful.

These, after all, were voices wanting to be heard-sometimes most desperately. 'I must talk with someone', wrote Kathleen Woodward.[49] Just think of Hannah Mitchell labouring over her autobiography in the Second World War, declaring her continuing faith in socialism and in a woman's right 'to her individuality, her own soul'.[50] Her consciousness of class and gender was the result of thought and of experience:

> I still crave for leisure, still long for solitude, still have a keen desire to learn. I love books, nature, the wild flowers, trees and hills of my native county which I rarely see. I still feel the urge to write, to express the impressions and experience and the dearly won knowledge of a fairly long and active life.[51]

The thwarted desire for self-expression of Hannah Mitchell and the other women whose stories entered history as personal narratives leave a moving indictment of forms of inequality which are not just about material things but about assumption and presumption. Great social changes have occurred since Virginia Woolf wrote her introduction to *Life As We Have Known It*. The dynamics of class have been transformed, yet subtle forms of inequality perpetuate unequal access to cultural space, suppressing the telling, the recording and the reception of the ideas and experience of working-class women.

Notes

* Bristol Broadsides, *Shush Mum's Writing* (Bristol, 1978).
1. Alice Clark, *Working Life of Women in the Seventeenth Century* (London, 1968).
2. See Paul Thompson (ed.), Our Common History. The transformation of history (London, 1982), pp.11–14; George Ewart Evans, *Spoken History* (London, 1987), pp.1–11, 88–9 and 141–150; Laurie Taylor, 'Diary' (on Charles Parker), *New Statesman and Society*, 23 June 1995, p.6.
3. Liz Heron (ed.), *Truth, Dare or Promise. Girls growing up in the 50s* (London, 1985), p.3.
4. Geoffrey Mitchell (ed.), *The Hard Way Up. The autobiography of Hannah Mitchell, suffragette and rebel* (London, 1977), p.96 (first published London, 1968).
5. Mitchell, *Hard Way Up*, p.217.
6. Geoffrey Mitchell, 'Introduction', in Mitchell, *Hard Way Up*, p.32.
7. See Sheila Rowbotham, 'Florence Exten-Hann: socialist and feminist', *Red Rag*, 5 (1973), reprinted in Sheila Rowbotham, *Dreams and Dilemmas. Collected writings* (London, 1983), pp.223–8.
8. Suzie Fleming and Gloden Dallas, 'Jessie' in Marsha Rowe (ed.), *Spare Rib Reader: 100 issues of women's liberation* (London, 1982), p.561.
9. Jill Liddington, 'Looking for Mrs Cooper', *North West Labour History Society Bulletin*, 7(1980-81), p.36.
10. Jean McCrindle and Sheila Rowbotham (eds), *Dutiful Daughters. Women talk about their lives* (London, 1979), p.9.
11. See Liz Heron, 'Giving people a voice', *The Times Educational Supplement*, 13 June 1980, p.19.
12. Margaret Powell, *Climbing the Stairs* (London, 1971), p.78 (first published London, 1969).
13. Virginia Woolf, 'Introduction', in Margaret Llewelyn Davies, *Life As We Have Known It* (London, 1931), p.xv.
14. Woolf, in Llewelyn Davies, *Life*, p.xxxvi.
15. Barbara Marsh, in McCrindle and Rowbotham, *Dutiful Daughters*, p.255.
16. Grace Foakes, *My Part of the River* (London, 1976), p.192 (first published in two volumes: *Between High Walls* (London, 1972) and *My Part of the River* (London, 1974).
17. Foakes, *River*, p.25.
18. Luisa Passerini, 'Work, ideology and working-class attitudes to Fascism', in Thompson, *Common History*, p.75.
19. Passerini, in Thompson, *Common History*, p.75.
20. Dot Starn, *When I Was a Child* (London, 1973), p.19.
21. Starn, *Child*, p.20.
22. Starn, *Child*, p.20.
23. Elizabeth Harrison, 'The needy not the greedy' in Durham Strong Words Collective (ed.), *But The World Goes On The Same. Changing times in Durham pit villages* (Whitley Bay, 1979), p.78.

24. Harrison, in Durham Strong Words Collective, *World*, p.80.
25. Merlin Clarke, 'Memories of my mother-in-law', in Rowe (ed.), *Spare Rib Reader*, p.139.
26. Clarke, in Rowe, *Spare Rib Reader*, p.139.
27. Foakes, *River*, p.109.
28. Daisy Noakes, *Faded Rainbow: Our married years* (Brighton, 1980), p.55.
29. Noakes, *Rainbow*, p.56.
30. Kathleen Woodward, *Jipping Street* (London, 1983), p.19.
31. Woodward, *Jipping Street*, pp.19–20.
32. Maggie Fuller, in McCrindle and Rowbotham, *Dutiful Daughters*, p.116.
33. Mitchell, *Hard Way Up*, pp.42–3.
34. Sally Alexander, 'Becoming a woman in London in the 1920s and '30s', in Sally Alexander, *Becoming a Woman and Other Essays in 19th and 20th Century Feminist History* (London, 1994), p.205.
35. Jean Mormont, in McCrindle and Rowbotham, *Dutiful Daughters*, pp.140–1.
36. Linda Peffer, in McCrindle and Rowbotham, *Dutiful Daughters*, p.366.
37. Maggie Fuller, in McCrindle and Rowbotham, *Dutiful Daughters*, p.124.
38. Annie Davison, in McCrindle and Rowbotham, *Dutiful Daughters*, p.73.
39. Annie Williams, in McCrindle and Rowbotham, *Dutiful Daughters*, p.38.
40. Noakes, *Rainbow*, p.5.
41. Fleming and Dallas, in Rowe, *Spare Rib Reader*, p.560.
42. Fleming and Dallas, in Rowe, *Spare Rib Reader*, p.560.
43. Woodward, *Jipping Street*, p.83.
44. Llewelyn Davies, *Life*, p.76.
45. Foakes, *River*, p.145.
46. Vera Alsop, in Durham Strong Words Collective, *World*, p.71.
47. Alsop, in Durham Strong Words Collective, *World*, p.71.
48. Alsop, in Durham Strong Words Collective, *World*, p.72.
49. Woodward, *Jipping Street*, p.151.
50. Mitchell, *Hard Way Up*, p.242.
51. Mitchell, *Hard Way Up*, p.240.

'The Immense Meaning of it All'
The challenges of internationalism for British socialist women before the First World War

Karen Hunt

Internationalism was an important part of the rhetoric of socialism and the women's movement. This article is concerned with what internationalism meant to socialist women, in particular, and how this translated into their politics. Although some attention has been given to reclaiming the history of the women's/suffrage internationals[1] to add to the existing histories of the Socialist Internationals,[2] there is little space in either literature for the specific experiences of socialist women. This might be because socialist women did not have an experience which was distinct from either, on the one hand, other socialists or, on the other hand, from other suffragists. Yet the evidence suggests that to be a woman in the Socialist International usually meant marginality whilst to raise socialist issues within the women's internationals was equally difficult. The focus here is therefore to consider the extent to which internationalism united British socialist women across their respective parties, both organisationally and rhetorically, and how this played out over time.

From the last quarter of the nineteenth century up to the First World War, there were a number of transnational organisations in which British socialist women might become involved. The Second International (1889–1914) provided a means for representatives of socialist parties from across the world (principally from Europe and the United States) to meet and formulate guiding, if not binding, policy. From 1907 the congresses of the Second International were prefaced by international meetings of socialist women with their own supporting inter-congress organisation. The women's movement also sought to make links across national boundaries, eventually formalising these links in a number of transnational organisations. Before the First World War these were the International Council of Women (ICW) founded in 1888 and the International Woman Suffrage Alliance (IWSA) formed in 1904. In many ways the socialist and women's internationals were parallel universes, with no organisational links between them. Socialist women were, it seems, expected to choose between their socialism and their commitment to a woman-centred politics[3] yet individual socialist women can be found taking part in the deliberations of both the socialist and the women's internationals. Were these women exceptions? How does their experience enable us to understand what internationalism meant to socialist women? Discerning a gendered reading of internationalism is not helped by the fact that internationalism itself was so little interrogated by socialists in general while the tension between it and nationalism and/or patriotism was too often ignored.

Interrogating internationalism

Despite the ubiquity of internationalism amongst socialists before the First World War, very little attention was given to defining the term itself. Certainly Ramsay MacDonald was not the only socialist who might be described, in Marquand's terms, as an 'instinctive internationalist'. MacDonald

> spoke no foreign languages apart from a little French, he liked foreigners and got on well with them; and it is clear from his travel writings that he felt a sense of excitement and liberation when he went abroad. Unlike many of his countrymen, he did not find it shocking or outrageous that foreigners should sometimes question Britain's motives or act in a way that did not conform to Britain's interests. At a deeper level still, he loathed violence and threats of violence.[4]

Amongst British male socialists, MacDonald was one of the more active participants in the Second International congresses and in the politics of internationalism. Does his rather vague version of internationalism, premised as much on delight in travel and 'foreigners' as any explicit sense of international solidarity, tell us anything about the models of internationalism open to socialist women of the same period? Maybe it was this rather amorphous internationalism which the Social Democratic Federation executive was criticising when it spoke in 1904 of an undifferentiated internationalism, a 'sort of gigantic steam roller', which was counterposed to their position of support for the 'the old Liberal tradition of the rights of little people'.[5] Here there is some suggestion that the tension between nationalism and internationalism is an uncomfortable one in which there is no desire to obliterate the nationalist struggles of the colonised. Certainly, some socialists expressed internationalist sentiments which included unambiguous anti-imperialist views, although these were often presented in a highly rhetorical form.[6] Perhaps the individual most thoroughly identified with internationalism in pre-war British socialist politics was Keir Hardie, who was described by Philip Snowden as having 'in a larger measure than, perhaps, any other man I have known...the international heart and mind'.[7] Although often represented as a sentimental commitment to international brotherhood, Kenneth Morgan maintains that Hardie's internationalism 'was always hedged around by realism; it was never *merely* sentimental'.[8] He saw the International as 'a kind of world-wide equivalent of the Labour Representation Committee at home, where different ideologies would be expressed, and reconciled gradually, through discussion, tolerance and pragmatic reform'.[9] His was an internationalism which centred on fraternity—was this therefore an internationalism which had space for socialist women or did some socialist women feel the need to create a more woman-focused version?

Another possible influence on socialist women's conception of internationalism might be found in the women's/suffrage transnational organisations. Leila Rupp has shown how here too definitions of internationalism were never rigorous: 'internationalism remained a vaguely defined force'.[10] Attempting to balance the pull of national loyalties with the aspiration of internationalism, this early generation of women internationalists would have agreed with Carrie Chapman Catt's view that internationalism was 'a sentiment like love, or religion, or patriotism, which is to be experienced rather than defined in words'.[11] Rupp suggests that rather than ignoring their differences, particularly but not exclusively national differences, the women of the ICW and IWSA conceptualised internationalism 'as a stitched together quilt of existing differences rather than a wholly new piece of cloth. Unity came out of merging diversity'.[12] Yet, as will become apparent, some of these differences over suffrage and especially between socialist women and the women's transnational organisations became too profound to be accommodated even within the metaphor of a patchwork quilt. Historians of the Irish women's movement have noted how for Irish women this 'patchwork quilt of differences' did not give the nationalists amongst them sufficient recognition of the centrality of nationalism to their understanding of internationalism.[13] Nevertheless, Minneke Bosch has argued that the IWSA 'lent reality to the idea of an essential unity and equality of women by the use of a recurring set of gripping images around notions of difference—in fact by exaggerating differences and romanticizing them'.[14] This was particularly apparent in the many national reports which were made to the Congresses, where a delegate often in national costume emphasised the particularity of her national or even regional experience whilst 'at the same time asserting solidarity, equality, and unity of principle'.[15] For socialist women internationalists, it was their socialism, their participation in mixed-sex organisations and their adult suffragism which were to be a difference too far for the pre-war transnational women's organisations. For British socialist women within the Second International the potential points of fracture for their internationalism were suffrage politics and party loyalty. It is an assessment of the relative importance of all these differences to British socialist women aspiring to a universalistic internationalism which forms the subject of this article.

British women and the Second International

The histories of the Second International give very little space to women's participation and to the meaning of internationalism to socialist women. Amongst the variety of socialisms which existed in Britain before the First World War, all made some commitment to internationalism at the level of rhetoric although the relationship between this and a sense of national identity, and even nationalism, was both awkward and largely unexplored. Internationalism certainly seems to have been an important aspect of the socialism of many British women. This could take in a range of different practices, from the rhetorical flourish; through travel and correspondence, networking with sisters and comrades from across the globe; sharing experiences and propagandising around the struggles and achievements of women and workers in other countries; to the participation in formal international congresses and their supporting national organisations.

The most visible sign of a commitment to internationalism was attendance at an international congress. Indeed, in the early years of the Second International before the formation of the International Socialist Bureau (1900) the only real opportunity for any socialist, whether man or woman, to formally express their internationalism was to be a delegate, speaker, translator or organiser at a congress. Women's participation rates were generally very low and the British delegations were no exception. On the one occasion when the International's Congress was held within Britain—in London in 1896—many British socialist women were able to attend for the first and last time.[16] Although there was a slow increase in women's attendance at the congresses held in continental Europe, it was rare to hear a woman speak, particularly a British one. Such low levels of participation were not unusual for socialist conferences generally. Women never constituted as much as ten per cent of Social Democratic Federation (SDF) or Independent Labour

Party (ILP) Annual Conferences.[17] In comparison, Sozialdemokratische Partei Deutschlands (SPD) women, despite being considerably more numerous, formed only a fraction of their annual conferences, not even equalling the ILP's figures before 1908.[18] The usual reasons for women's under-representation were amplified for international congresses. The cost, travel and disruption to domestic life were greatly increased when attendance involved foreign travel. These were barriers to the participation of many working-class socialists, but it was particularly difficult for women, without an independent income or having domestic responsibilities, to become part of one of the British delegations to the international. Indeed, the general concern for costs was reflected in a discussion in the ILP's *Labour Leader* on the cheapest and quickest routes to Copenhagen for the International Congress in 1910.[19]

At national conferences many of the women who attended were accompanying their husbands, but there is less evidence of this among the British delegations to the International. Although Ramsay and Margaret MacDonald attended together not even all the well-known British partnerships took part in the Internationals, for example J. and Katherine Bruce Glasier. Responsibility for young children often precluded wives from accompanying their husbands on foreign travel, although not always, as Margaret MacDonald confided in a friend in 1904:

> my husband and I have been to the Amsterdam International Socialist Congress and found it immensely interesting. I had of course not expected to be able to go, but as I found that my nursing the baby did not agree with him I was not too tied to him as my mother-in-law was willing to look after him and the others, and let us both off.[20]

For these and other practical reasons, it is not surprising that, with the exception of the year that the congress was held in London, female delegates to the International were drawn from those who were virtually full-time political activists. Some of these women were mothers, but their political activism had already meant that they had had to make arrangements for childcare.[21] As if to remind delegates of the practical problems faced by socialist mothers, Margaret MacDonald attended the 1910 Congress when her pregnancy with her sixth child would have been evident to all.[22]

The limited number of British women attending international congresses was not an indication of socialist women's lack of interest in internationalism. For example, for those in the SDF, internationalism was an important part of their socialism. This has been obscured by the retrospective representation of the party as the creature of Hyndman,[23] with views synonymous with his. Women, in particular, may have been more internationally minded than many of their socialist brothers partly because they regarded the theory and practice of the SPD on the woman question as a positive model. Some women members of the SDF played an important role in sustaining their party's internationalism. For example, the international reports, which were always a feature of the SDF's newspaper *Justice*, relied heavily on the contributions of Eleanor Marx. The links between women in other parties of the Second International and those in the SDF were enhanced by personal networks. Eleanor Marx was an important early figure and by 1905 *Justice* was able to name three women in particular as 'home grown Social Democrats [who] enjoy great and world-wide reputations'—Dora Montefiore, Rose Jarvis and Charlotte Despard.[24] Of these, the most important for SDF women on the international scene was undoubtedly Dora Montefiore.[25] She was a friend of Clara Zetkin and Alexandra Kollontai. They were part of an international network of socialist women whose mutual friendship helped to reinforce a pre-existing commitment to internationalism.

The journalism of internationally minded socialist women ensured that the practical effect of international congresses for their participants was shared with a wider domestic audience. Margaret MacDonald and Mary Middleton looked forward to the 1910 Socialist Women's International Congress as they hoped it 'will increase the possibilities of exchanging informations and suggestions between those who are working for the same cause in different parts of the world'. For those who had no prospect of attending such a gathering the international reports included, for example, in 'Our Women's Column' in *Justice* provided an inspiration. One woman SDFer welcomed news of 'the organised fight of the working women in those lands against the forces of tyranny and reaction. We recognise that we are one with them, and our hearts rejoice'.[26] Internationalist aspirations could be sustained at a distance and without ever having to leave home.

Justice was not the only socialist paper whose women's column gave coverage to events within the international socialist movement. *Labour Leader* also gave space to international events as did *Labour Woman*, latterly under the title 'Our Sisters Abroad'. ILP women also had international connections although they do not seem to have been part of friendship networks in quite the same way as Dora Montefiore. Margaret MacDonald was an assiduous attender of international congresses 'though most of the leading Socialist women of the Continent were against her'.[27] The ILP women's experience of the International is largely explained by the difference in their conception of socialism compared with the Second International's Marxism. Their isolation within the International, particularly the Socialist Women's

International, was compounded by the ILP's support for a limited women's franchise (votes on the same terms as men, i.e. a property-based franchise) in opposition to the International's advocacy of adult suffrage (votes for all adult women and men). Moreover, although the different approaches of SDF and ILP women within the International must be set within the context of the politics of the divided parent British section, nevertheless, in such relatively confined circles the personal relationships of the women concerned could colour their strategies. Certainly, there is little evidence that Margaret MacDonald and Dora Montefiore were able to put behind them the 'Belt Affair'[28] of 1899 and the subsequent libel case in their years of participation within the Socialist Women's International. Although the strain between Margaret MacDonald and Dora Montefiore clearly did affect relationships between other socialist women it would be wrong to see this as taking the form of a straightforward SDF/ILP divide or that it was itself responsible for polarising the relationship between SDF and ILP women. Individuals such as Margaret Bondfield worked with both groups.[29]

British socialist women and the Socialist Women's International

I now want to turn to the ways in which British women organised in relation to the Second International to see what this reveals about the tensions within their internationalist politics. To what extent were British socialist women able to create an internationalist practice which could accommodate domestic differences?

The first meeting of the Socialist Women's International was held immediately before the full international congress in Stuttgart in 1907. It was a largely female event controlled by women and provided the first formal opportunity for socialist women to meet within the setting of the international. Kathleen Kough of the SDF found this first congress 'a revelation and an inspiration'.[30] Many of the British socialist women who had previously attended international congresses now found they had an opportunity to speak and eagerly joined in the deliberations of the women's congress. The British delegation was particularly vocal in the suffrage debate because they were such a divided group. This division was apparent from the start of the congress when the SDFer Dora Montefiore's credentials to take part in the meeting were challenged by other British women comrades. The ostensible grounds were that the Adult Suffrage Society, which she was representing, was not a socialist organisation. As the ILP objectors were supporters of limited women's suffrage it seems more likely that they were trying to prevent the British case being made for adult suffrage. Their objections were overruled by Clara Zetkin and the conference voted to accept Montefiore's credentials.[31] Although this was all done 'in a perfectly friendly spirit',[32] according to the *Clarion*, it was at least an ironic gesture and probably explicit revenge by ILPers for the challenges made by the SDF within the International to the socialist credentials of the Labour Party.

With her credentials to attend the conference recognised, Dora Montefiore was able to participate in the suffrage debate where she and Margaret MacDonald once again came into conflict. MacDonald accused Montefiore of preventing her from making the case for limited suffrage to the women's congress.[33] Despite the objections of some of the British delegation, the women's congress voted overwhelmingly in favour of adult suffrage. This debate showed a divided British women's delegation whose differences were carried over into the full congress's debate on suffrage. As we shall see, suffrage was also a crucial and divisive issue for those British socialist women who participated in the women's internationals. At the second Socialist Women's Congress in 1910 suffrage was again an issue which caused bad feeling within the British delegation. As Margaret MacDonald told readers of *Labour Leader*:

> We should not mind the majority pronouncing against limited suffrage if they would recognise the right of any country to use different tactics without being called bad names, but when one has heard misrepresentations made by Mrs Dora Montefiore (who, according to her associations, herself 'insulted her sex' by going to prison for a day or two once for the WSPU) and other SDP representatives this year, and three years ago, one must have patience with some misconceptions on the part of foreign comrades.[34]

MacDonald's exasperated tone continued in her report of the congress when she described some confusion over the calling of speakers from the British delegation:

> As both this year and three years ago, the WLL [Women's Labour League], ILP and Fabian women had already, for the sake of letting things go smoothly, put up quietly with much more of Mrs Montefiore than is justified by her influence or representative character in the British movement, and as Mrs Montefiore smilingly assured me, when I appealed to her to have the common courtesy to let one of us move our own League resolutions, that she would speak about them for us in the course of her speech, we felt it was time to make a public protest, and we walked out of the hall in a body.[35]

Here differences in party and suffrage politics were exacerbated by personal differences as ILP and SDF women jostled to be the voice of British socialist women and to mould the Socialist Women's International to their views on the contentious issue of suffrage.

The first Socialist Women's Congress also called for the formation of an International Bureau for Socialist Women to mirror the functions of the International Socialist Bureau (ISB); that is to maintain communication between national sections and to promote the implementation of the International's decisions. Just as the SPD dominated the full International so their large and successful women's organisation was the key to formalising the international network of socialist women. The political and personal differences within the British section of the International have been traced by Douglas Newton[36] but there is no analysis within his work of the equivalent British women's organisation. Nor has the effect of the rivalry between the ILP and the SDF on British participation in the International been examined from the perspective of socialist women. As we have already seen the British section of the Socialist Women's International was as riven with divisions as were the British delegations to the full International.

The meeting to set up Britain's own women's section of the International was called by SDF women. The Socialist Women's Bureau (British) included representatives from the SDF and its Women's Committee, the Fabian Society, Clarion Scouts, Teachers' Association and the Adult Suffrage Society. However the absence of women from the ILP and WLL meant that the group came to be seen as an SDF organisation to be marginalised by mainstream labour and socialist women. For its part, the SDF sought to involve the ILP and to broaden the base of the Bureau.[37] These overtures were largely unsuccessful, despite the fact that it was hard to represent the Bureau as purely a creature of the SDF.

The initial object of the Socialist Women's Bureau (British) was to establish regular communication between the organised socialist women of all countries, and thereby to illustrate the virtues of internationalism. Unfortunately communication within Britain was to be more problematic, although the bureau stressed it sought to be as representative as possible. The Bureau also began a comparative investigation of international social policy, such as the provision of maternity pensions. It also sponsored public meetings such as the visit of Clara Zetkin and Alexandra Kollontai in 1909. Although the key issue of 'women and war' was discussed by the Bureau, it did not tackle the topic which had so divided the British women's delegation at Stuttgart: the suffrage. But then adult suffrage was an uncontentious position for most of those who chose to be involved in the Bureau.

Thus the Socialist Women's Bureau from 1907 to 1910 seems to have achieved at least as much as the equivalent men's organisation.[38] Yet part of the purpose of the national sections was to encourage socialist unity and to stop inter-party squabbling. Here success was much more limited and the Socialist Women's Bureau should be seen as part of the jostling between the ILP and SDF for leadership of the British presence within the International.

In 1910 the balance of forces changed. At the second Socialist Women's International Congress in Copenhagen the British delegation was again divided over suffrage. But the congress as a whole was somewhat overshadowed by the struggle between the SDP, as the SDF had been re-christened in 1908, and the ILP. Bruce Glasier reported triumphantly that at the Stuttgart Conference 'the SDP delegates were able to have things all their own way, at Copenhagen they had to submit to the overpowering vote of the ILP and the two other groups, an experience of democratic rule which they hotly resented'.[39] Moreover, the WLL was now determined to wrest the Bureau from the hands of the SDP. Consequently, after the Copenhagen Congress, the League decided to call a fresh conference to form a British women's section. Effectively the ILP women seized the initiative and succeeded in establishing a new organisation—the Women's International Council of Socialist and Labour Organisations (British Section)—dominated by their own members.

The changing personnel and activities of this new organisation can be monitored through *Fabian News*, the *League Leaflet* and later *Labour Woman*. Since the activities of the Women's International Council were not markedly different from that of the Bureau, it seems that ILP women were more interested in taking control for its own sake. The main thing was to marginalise the SDP. But factors outside the immediate control of SDP women ensured that the WLL was never seriously challenged within the Women's International Council. Maybe it did not seem to matter so much any more: with Margaret MacDonald dead and Dora Montefiore outside the British Socialist Party (BSP)—successor to the SDP—from the end of 1912 and travelling abroad, two of the main protagonists were no longer part of the picture. The SDP Women's Committee was dissolved at the beginning of 1912 as part of the move to establish the BSP. Although there were attempts to get the BSP to affiliate to the Women's International Council in late 1912, their affiliation was not confirmed until mid-1914.[40] Moreover, the truncated and hastily arranged international congress at Basle in 1912 did not reawaken feelings of internationalism amongst British socialist women, despite its theme of peace. With the outbreak of the First World War, the Second International shattered as SPD deputies voted for war credits and the force of national allegiances splintered the fragile rhetoric of internationalism. The Women's International Council did, however, continue to operate during the war, keeping in touch with working women in other countries and holding pro-peace meetings as well as taking part in the Socialist Women's Congress in Berne in 1915.

Thus British women contributed to the operation of the Second International and shared its aspirations but in a way which was constrained by the Second International's understanding of the woman question. Just as the constituent parties had an ambivalent relationship to the semi-autonomous organisation of socialist women within their national party structures, so the Second International itself allowed women space to organise but not the power to influence its deliberations. British women's organisation in relation to the International was further constrained by the relationship between their parent parties. By 1907, and the establishment of the Socialist Women's International, the relationship between British socialist women, formally and informally, was already marked by the differences in emphases of their socialism. In addition to this, they had their own personal and political divisions, particularly over the suffrage.

Socialist women and the women's internationals

Despite the Second International's characterisation of autonomous women's organisations as 'bourgeois', many socialist women took part, sometimes critically and often ambivalently, in women's and women's suffrage organisations within Britain. In some cases this was translated into an activism which crossed national borders and which was fuelled by a commitment to a woman-focused internationalism.

The socialist press did not give systematic or even consistent coverage to the women's/women's suffrage internationals. Unsurprisingly, the fact that the 1899 International Women's Congress was held in London meant both a greater involvement of British women, including socialist women, and also a greater interest from the press. *Labour Leader* and *Clarion* both noted that the congress involved 'a great many socialists'.[41] The issues raised in the socialist press coverage were the thorny ones for socialists—sex versus class. *Labour Leader* gave the fullest account of the congress choosing to emphasise that although this was called a 'women's congress' a significant number of the speakers were men and the President, Lady Aberdeen, had said in her opening address:

> many of those present felt with herself that the banding together of

women apart from men must be regarded in most cases as a temporary expedient to meet a temporary need, and that it must not be allowed to crystallise into a permanent element in social life.[42]

Amongst the wide range of papers given over the course of the congress, *Labour Leader* mentioned a contribution from the socialist Mrs Bridges Adams who 'said that the emancipation of women was doomed to failure unless it ceased to be a sex movement and became part of the great effort on behalf of adult suffrage'.[43] This summed up what was to be the basis of the rather uncomfortable relationship that many socialist women had with the women's/women's suffrage internationals: the apparent privileging of gender over class and the priority given to limited women's suffrage rather than adult suffrage. Because of the latter it was easier for ILP suffragists (many of whom were committed to limited women's suffrage, working either as part of the constitutional National Union of Women's Suffrage Societies [NUWSS] or the militant Women's Social and Political Union [WSPU]) rather than SDF suffragists (amongst whom adult suffrage was the dominant position) to take part in the congresses of the IWSA. Thus Isabella Ford of the ILP regularly attended IWSA congresses until her death in 1924 while the right of the SDFer Dora Montefiore to attend the same conferences was continually challenged.

In observing that 'the most troubling gap for those who longed for unity of women was the chasm that yawned between the bourgeois and socialist women's movements', Leila Rupp has suggested that the blame for this resides with socialist women.[44] Because socialist women refused an invitation to participate in the 1904 ICW Congress and because the Socialist Women's International rejected any cooperation across political lines, the worlds of organised socialist women and the transnational women's organisations barely touched. Yet from the perspective of socialist women, not only are the examples cited by Rupp hardly decisive, the women's internationals could be less than welcoming not only to the organisations of socialist women but also to individual socialist women. Amongst the British socialist women the experience of Dora Montefiore was the most extreme example. After the 1899 ICW Congress in London, British socialist women who participated in women's transnational organisations put their energies into the IWSA. So after having been part of the organising committee for the ICW Congress in 1899 (not uncomplicatedly—she was removed from her post because Margaret MacDonald had told the President of the ICW that scandal was associated with Montefiore), Dora Montefiore attended a series of IWSA congresses. Her right to participate was challenged because the only group who could officially represent Britain were the constitutionalist advocates of limited women's suffrage, the NUWSS. When Dora Montefiore attended the IWSA Congress in 1906 in Copenhagen, she did so as a representative of the WSPU. Despite a challenge to her credentials to address the congress from within the official British delegation, the President of the IWSA ruled in Montefiore's favour.[45] From 1907 Dora Montefiore was a member of the Adult Suffrage Society,[46] while remaining a leading member of the SDF. Not only were her conference credentials challenged at the Socialist Women's Congress in 1907 because of her adult suffragism, but also she was challenged for the same reason at the IWSA Congress in London in 1909. These challenges were all made by other British delegates, revealing the extent of differences among socialist women and among suffragist women as well as between them. Although Dora Montefiore persisted in trying to find a space for herself as an adult suffragist within the IWSA, the leadership sought to distance themselves from her. This was revealed in letters between two IWSA activists, Aletta Jacobs and Rosika Schwimmer:

> Mrs Montefiore is now working in the socialist party, who are against Wom.Suffrage[sic]. She wrote Martina and me lately, that she will only work for adult suffrage and against ladies-suffrage. Martina and I found it a good moment to write her that both of us preferred not to receive more letters. Our correspondence could only be disagreeable for both parties…[47]

The offence seems to be her adult suffragism but also her socialism. Ironically, the Martina mentioned here is Martina Kramers, also a socialist and suffragist, who was to find herself driven from the IWSA—in her case the reason given was the supposed scandal she brought in her wake because of her long relationship with a married socialist man. Despite focusing on issues of propriety, there is some suggestion that the real offence might have been too great an affinity with socialism.[48] There are at least some echoes here of some of the difficulties experienced by Montefiore in being a socialist and a suffragist within a women's transnational organisation.

It was as a consequence of the 1909 IWSA Congress—and Montefiore's treatment at it—that Clara Zetkin made explicit the attitude of organised socialist women to the IWSA. She made clear that Montefiore had only taken part in the congress 'with the definite object only of compelling the Alliance to give a decisive and clear declaration on the issue, 'Women's or Ladies' Franchise', so that there could no longer remain any doubt as to its aim'.[49]

When Dora Montefiore and the other representatives of the ASS found their right to participate in the congress challenged, they walked out. Clara Zetkin said that this revealed the IWSA as 'the buttress of the possessing class against equal political rights for the whole of the female sex.... In naked ugliness it now stands, as the embodiment of narrow class interests, and as the aspiration of propertied women for a political monopoly'.[50]

Yet other British socialist women did not experience the IWSA as either explicitly anti-socialist or as resistant to their particular combination of socialist, suffrage and internationalist politics. Although *The Times* reported of the IWSA in 1908, 'Socialist women are not supporting the congress', Isabella Ford (ILPer and advocate of limited suffrage) saw IWSA congresses rather differently. In 1909 she reported:

> The chief thing which struck me during the women's International Congress in London, and which was remarkable also in the Congress last year in Amsterdam, was this, that the general drift of our movement is towards Socialism. Not always avowedly or consciously so by any means.[51]

She compared the IWSA with socialist and trade union congresses:

> In none I heard expressed a more complete understanding of the world's deep need of freedom—freedom for men as much as for women, a freedom which can only come when women have power to help men to reach it. At no Congress, too, have I felt the solidarity of the countries to be so strong...It is true that Socialism has watered and quickened the roots of our movement, but now, in return, it is we who want to lead the way to attain the most enduring and widest kind of Socialism. Till women are free men can never be free.[52]

Yet before we conclude that unlike Dora Montefiore, Isabella Ford *was* able to juggle the socialist and women's internationals successfully, it is important to note that although Ford attended international trade union congresses she was not involved in the Socialist Women's International. In her internationalist practice she chose to put her energies into the IWSA, while domestically she prioritised her suffragism over her socialism in her day-to-day work while never abandoning her ILP membership. Other socialist women still, like Ethel Snowden, could not even accept Ford's compromise. Snowden abandoned her ILP membership in 1909 in order to concentrate exclusively on the suffrage through the NUWSS. She was therefore not a formal member of a socialist party when she attended the IWSA Congress in 1911.[53]

Fabian women were also to be found attending IWSA Congresses. In 1909 they were fraternal delegates and reported that many of the congress participants were avowed socialists, indeed the majority of delegates were in favour of adult suffrage as the ultimate aim although the congress was united in regarding the sex barrier as the first obstacle to be overcome.[54] But maybe their reading of the IWSA arose from their location as moderate socialists and suffragists rather than from any shift in the intrinsic nature of the IWSA itself. Fabian women also attended the IWSA Congress in 1913 in Budapest. Their version of socialism and suffragism did not seem to make the IWSA an unsympathetic arena although they were hardly central to its deliberations. Nevertheless, Fabian women's politics seems to have been more acceptable: a version of socialism which did not stress class conflict and a suffragism which largely remained aligned with the NUWSS.

Clearly, then, British socialist women had different experiences of the relative inclusiveness of women's transnational organisations. British socialist women's kind of internationalism changed over time, and as women's positions on the suffrage polarised and socialist women's politics became more clearly differentiated from so called 'bourgeois feminism', it became harder to make links between the two worlds of women's and socialist internationalism. This is ironic in some respects as the subject matter of the ICW and IWSA was often very close to that of the Socialist Women's International and its British section—social reform, particularly linked to the family, maternity, children and childcare were topics which brought women's interests together, as did anti-militarism. Yet women were divided by the politics of their parent organisations; socialist women were distinguished from non-socialists, and even SDF from ILP women. The desire to achieve international solidarity between women remained but differences on strategies and priorities became sharper. Socialist women were marked as much by their membership of particular socialist parties as they were by their gender.

A socialist women's internationalism?

Many British socialist women were internationalists and the activists amongst them saw their formal relationship to the Second International as important enough to try and ensure that their own political perspective dominated. Within the confines of Second International socialism, a number of British women espoused and practised a woman-focused internationalism. What did this mean? This could be an inclusive but class-based internationalism. Thus, for example:

> It is...more than ever necessary that the working woman in England should learn solidarity with her working sisters in other lands, and should realise that it is not by alliances and compromises with the women of the master class that the hope of the workers will be realised, but by conscious and practical fellowship with the workers of other lands.[55]

This contrasts with, for example, the President of the ICW's understanding of internationalism, where:

> the very essence of the Council idea...is to provide a common centre for women workers of every race, faith, class and party, who are associating themselves together in the endeavour to leave the world better and more beautiful than they have found it.[56]

But it also contrasts with the emphases of ILP women who tended to downplay the class solidarity element in their internationalism. Thus Margaret MacDonald and Mary Middleton, speaking for the WLL, reported that their members:

> feel that international co-operation between women of similar sympathies is one of the most important parts of our work....By means of correspondence, and by inviting visitors to this country to their meetings, they are able to keep in touch with the women of the British Colonies and all foreign countries.[57]

Here internationalism is seen in rather similar terms to the example cited earlier of Keir Hardie. It provided opportunities for practical networking rather than making what were seen as overly ideological claims.

Yet despite these differences of emphasis it was the language of comradeship rather than that of sisterhood which was the orthodoxy. Nevertheless a number of the more enthusiastic internationalist socialist women claimed to be inspired by a sense of sisterhood, albeit undefined. For some it was possible to refuse the choice, thus Isabella Ford saw sisterhood as a compliment to, rather than a replacement for, the comradeship of the sexes.[58] For others the optimistic claim to sisterhood became increasingly discordant with their experience of the international woman's movement, thus in 1904 Dora Montefiore greeted the ICW/IWSA Congress as giving 'to women working all over the world in the cause of their sister women a feeling of solidarity and of sisterhood such as they never possessed before!'.[59] Later her language of sisterhood was replaced by a different emphasis; by 1909 she was arguing 'in helping forward the development of women we are helping forward the development of the race'.[60] Indeed, what drew socialist women together was an assumption that internationalism meant the solidarity of the human race rather then the feminists' stress on the solidarity of a sex. Sustaining a woman-focused politics was crucial to many British socialist women but this did not need to be a separatist activity, hence the endorsement of a solidarity based on the human race as a whole rather than on one sex. This was the context for Dora Montefiore's comment that, 'In internationalism...lies our hope for the future, for enlarged culture, for the spread of free thought, and for the realisation of the solidarity of the human race'[61] as it was for *Labour Leader*'s view of the 1913 IWSA Congress—'It is an earnest of the day when not merely the sex but the Humanity of Woman shall be recognised.'[62] It was this desire to find a way to make a mixed-sex politics work for women socialists which explains some of the suspicion of activists in the single-sex IWSA towards socialist women. As Rupp has noted of Martina Kramers and others (although interestingly not Dora Montefiore), IWSA critics 'linked the aberrant heterosexual relationships to political work with men and seemed to disapprove of both'.[63]

The other aspect of the internationalism of British socialist women before the First World War which deserves exploration is its relationship to imperialism. Antoinette Burton has revealed that 'If suffrage was marked as an imperialized discourse in the early twentieth century, it remained, as it had been in the Victorian period, egalitarian and international in its rhetoric as well'.[64] These apparent contradictions might also be observed in relation to socialists of the same period. Although some British socialist women did show some awareness of the issues: Isabella Ford felt, in relation to the 1909 IWSA Congress, that 'the feeling of our common womanhood wiped out racial feeling as I have never before seen it wiped out'.[65] Dora Montefiore aspired to 'place fellowship above competitive imperialism'[66] for by 1911 she was clear that 'International Socialism unites on the basis of THE CLASS STRUGGLE, NOT COLOUR OR SEX STRUGGLE'.[67] But these were not the dominant views of socialists more generally or socialist women in particular. In Montefiore's case the evolution of her internationalism seems to have been directly affected by her unusual experience of extensive international travel and working with socialists and suffragists particularly in the United States and the White Dominions of the British Empire (specifically Australia and South Africa).[68]

If little time was spent by British socialist women, either domestically or internationally, in discussing what they understood by 'internationalism', those that experienced international gatherings were convinced that they understood the meaning and importance of internationalism. One of the British women delegates to the 1910 meeting of the Socialist Women's International commented:

> I hope never to miss an International Socialist Congress again. I am just realising what a big thing it is in which we have taken part. Whilst it is going on it sometimes seems weary and ineffective, but when one sees the delegates all gathered together like this one feels the enthusiasm and the immense meaning of it all.[69]

The 'immense meaning' of internationalism to socialist women before the First World War is hard to decipher. Could the aspiration of an inclusive internationalism override socialist women's other loyalties? In the organisational context of conferences and meetings, party could be an obstacle to harmonious relations but specific issues were equally divisive, particularly suffrage. Yet there was a strong desire to learn from the experience of women across the world and to feel part of something bigger than the nation state. The rhetoric of internationalism was an important way in which a divided movement (divided by party and by sex) could feel it was moving in the same direction. Solidarity with other national workers' and women's movements was some times easier than with other competing organisations within one's own country.

Just as building a distinct and coherent woman-focused socialism was more of an aspiration than a reality, so many of the Edwardian generation of socialist women took it for granted that internationalism was an essential part of their politics. But, like their male comrades, socialist women rarely explored the detail of what internationalism meant as a practical politics or reflected on the challenge that the aspiration of internationalism posed to socialism in the years before the First World War.

Notes

1. E.F. Hurwitz, 'The international sisterhood', in R. Bridenthal and C. Koonz (eds), *Becoming Visible. Women in European history* (Boston, 1977); R.L. Sherrick, 'Toward universal sisterhood', *Women's Studies International Forum*, vol. 5, no. 6 (1982); L.J. Rupp, 'Constructing Internationalism. The case of transnational women's organizations, 1888–1945', *American Historical Review*, no. 99 (1994); A. Burton, *Burdens of History. British feminists, Indian women, and imperial culture, 1865–1915* (Chapel Hill, 1994), ch. 6; E.C. Dubois, 'Woman suffrage around the world. Three phases of suffragist internationalism', in C. Daley and M. Nolan (eds), *Suffrage and Beyond. International feminist perspectives* (Auckland, 1994);

1. L.J. Rupp, *Worlds of Women. The making of an international women's movement* (Princeton, 1997).
2. G.D.H. Cole, *The Second International, 1889–1914* (London, 1956); J. Joll, *The Second International, 1889–1914* (London, 1974).
3. For a different interpretation of the relationship between the socialist and women's internationals see E.C. Dubois, 'Woman Suffrage and the Left. An international socialist-feminist perspective' in her *Woman Suffrage and Women's Rights* (New York, 1998), pp.252–82.
4. D. Marquand, *Ramsay MacDonald* (London, 1997; first published 1977) pp.164–5.
5. *Social Democrat*, April 1904, quoted in C. Tsuzuki, *Hyndman and British Socialism* (Oxford, 1961), p.194.
6. See, for example, the discussion of Belfort Bax in B. Baker, 'The Social Democratic Federation and the Boer War', *Our History*, vol. 59 (1974), pp.4–5.
7. P. Snowden, quoted in K.O. Morgan, *Keir Hardie. Radical and socialist* (London, 1975), p.178.
8. Ibid., p.179.
9. Ibid., p.180.
10. Rupp, *Worlds of Women*, p.108.
11. Carrie Chapman Catt speaking to 1909 IWSA Congress, quoted in Rupp, *Worlds of Women*, p.108.
12. Ibid., pp.108–9.
13. M. Ward, 'Nationalism, pacifism, internationalism. Louie Bennett, Hanna Sheehy-Skeffington, and the problems of "defining feminism"', in A. Bradley and M. Valiulis (eds), *Gender & Sexuality in Modern Ireland* (Amherst, MA, 1997); L. Ryan, 'A question of loyalty: War, nation, and feminism in early twentieth-century Ireland', *Women's Studies International Forum*, vol. 20, no. 1 (1997).
14. M. Bosch with A. Kloosterman (eds), *Politics and Friendship. Letters from the International Woman Suffrage Alliance, 1902–42* (Columbus, OH, 1990), p.18.
15. Ibid.
16. *List of British and Foreign Delegates and Balance Sheet* (London, 1896).
17. See Appendix 2 in K. Hunt, *Equivocal Feminists. The Social Democratic Federation and the woman question, 1884–1911* (Cambridge, 1996), p.260. In 1908 the SDF changed its name to the Social Democratic Party.
18. K. Honeycutt, 'Clara Zetkin: A left-wing socialist and feminist in Wilhelmian Germany', PhD, Columbia University, 1975, p.291.
19. *Labour Leader*, 10 June 1910; 17 June 1910.
20. Margaret E. MacDonald to Lady Mary Murray, 25 October 1904, Margaret E. MacDonald personal correspondence, PRO 30/69/891.
21. See, for example, the MacDonalds' attitudes to childcare in J. Cox (ed.), *A Singular Marriage. A Labour love story in letters and diaries. Ramsay and Margaret MacDonald* (London, 1988), pp.311–12.
22. Sheila MacDonald was born on 7 December 1910, three months after the International Socialist Women's Congress held in Copenhagen on 26 and 27 August 1910.

23. See Tsuzuki, *Hyndman and British Socialism*. For an examination of the stereotype of the SDF, see Hunt, *Equivocal Feminists*, pp.7–17.
24. *Justice*, 22 April 1905.
25. For an exploration of Dora Montefiore's internationalism see K. Hunt, 'Internationalism in Practice. The politics of a British socialist and feminist before the First World War', paper presented to European Social Science History Conference, Amsterdam, March 1998.
26. *Justice*, 1 May 1909.
27. J.R. MacDonald, *Margaret Ethel MacDonald*, 4th edn (London, 1913) p.226.
28. The Belt case arose from gossip that Dora Montefiore had had an improper relationship with a married working-class man, George Belt, who had subsequently lost his job as an organiser for the ILP in Hull. Margaret MacDonald told this story to Lady Aberdeen (President of the ICW) and, as a result, Belt sued MacDonald for making the malicious statement that he had been dismissed from the ILP for immoral conduct. See C. Collette, 'Socialism and scandal: the sexual politics of the early labour movement', *History Workshop Journal*, vol. 23 (1987), pp.102–11.
29. See M. Bondfield, *A Life's Work* (London, 1948).
30. *Justice*, 7 September 1907.
31. *Clarion*, 23 August 1907; D.B. Montefiore, *From a Victorian to a Modern* (London, 1927), p.120.
32. *Clarion*, 23 August 1907.
33. Ibid.
34. *Labour Leader*, 9 September 1910.
35. Ibid.
36. D.J. Newton, *British Labour, European Socialism and the Struggle for Peace 1889–1914* (Oxford,1985).
37. *Justice*, 9 November 1907; Women's Labour League Executive Committee Minute Book, National Museum of Labour History, 19 October 1910.
38. The British section of the Second International, the British National Committee, was in practice a men's organisation but for the one attendance by Ethel Bentham (British National Committee Minutes, 17 February 1911).
39. *Labour Leader*, 16 September 1910.
40. *Socialist Record*, July 1914.
41. *Labour Leader*, 10 June 1899. See also *Clarion*, 25 February, 17 June 1899.
42. *Labour Leader*, 1 July 1899.
43. *Labour Leader*, 8 July 1899.
44. Rupp, *Worlds of Women*, p.34.
45. *Bulletin of Monthly Correspondence of the IWSA*, 15 September 1906.
46. For the context of Dora Montefiore's suffrage politics see K. Hunt, 'Journeying through suffrage: The politics of Dora Montefiore', in C. Eustance, J. Ryan and L. Ugolini (eds), *A Suffrage Reader. Charting directions in British suffrage history* (London, 2000).
47. A. Jacobs to R. Schwimmer, 16 December 1907, in Bosch with Kloosterman

(eds), *Politics and Friendship*, p.74.
48. See C. Chapman Catt to M. Kramers, 21 May 1913 and M. Kramers to C. Chapman Catt, 2 June 1913 in Bosch with Kloosterman (eds), *Politics and Friendship*, pp.126–9; Rupp, *Worlds of Women*, p.95. See also L.J. Rupp, 'Sexuality and politics in the early twentieth century. The case of the international women's movement', *Feminist Studies*, vol. 23, no. 3 (1997).
49. Extract from *Gleichheit*, 7 June 1909 translated in *Justice*, 3 July 1909.
50. Ibid.
51. *Labour Leader*, 1 July 1909.
52. Ibid.
53. *Common Cause*, 25 May 1911.
54. *Fabian News*, June 1909.
55. *Justice*, 9 January 1909.
56. The Countess of Aberdeen (ed.), *The International Congress of Women 1899*, vol. 1 (London, 1900), p.48.
57. *Reports to the Second International Conference of Socialist Women*, 1910, p.31.
58. J. Hannam, *Isabella Ford* (Oxford, 1989), p.130.
59. *New Age*, 28 July 1904.
60. *Justice*, 20 March 1909.
61. *New Age*, 19 October 1905.
62. *Labour Leader*, 12 June 1913.
63. Rupp, 'Sexuality and politics', p.594.
64. Burton, *Burdens of History*, p.172.
65. *Labour Leader*, 2 July 1909.
66. Montefiore, *From a Victorian*, p.192.
67. *International Socialist* (Sydney), 30 December 1911.
68. See Hunt, 'Internationalism in Practice'.
69. *Labour Leader*, 16 September 1910.

Labour's Africa and the Mau Mau Rebellion

Paul Kelemen

Important aspects of the Labour Party's thinking on colonialism in Africa are illustrated by its pronouncements on Kenya, in the period 1918 to the early 1960s. Due to Kenya's strategic position in relation to British interests in the Middle East and to its small, but influential, European settler population, it was frequently discussed in Parliament, in the press and in the policy formulating circles of the party. Moreover, the conflict between European and African communities in Kenya touched on something more than colonial policy: it was increasingly linked, from the late 1930s, to a general pattern of white-black relations. Thus when the Mau Mau rebellion broke out, in 1952, *The Times*'s Nairobi correspondent reported that it 'must be regarded as a phase in the struggle of African nationalism' but alluded to what might make it assume additional significance. It was, the reporter noted: 'the first time that such a movement has taken place on the very doorstep of European settlement'.[1] The subsequent public discourse, in Britain, on the Mau Mau rebellion was largely coded in terms of a confrontation between European civilisation and African primitiveness.

The development of Labour's policy towards Kenya is revealing, therefore, not only of the party's colonial policy but also of the way Labour ideologists responded to debates about 'race relations' and 'Africanness'. Throughout the 1920s, Labour Party declarations on Africa were formulated on the basis of trusteeship. This principle was embodied in the party's August 1917 *War Aims Memorandum*, which set down Labour's peacetime objectives. It proposed: 'Home rule when people attain the necessary stage of decolonisation' but, where this was not the case—and all Labour politicians subscribed to the view that Africans were not at that stage—their interest should be looked after by the European powers acting as trustees. There was a range of proposals from Labour figures about how the trusteeship should be conducted, most envisaging the colonial power being answerable to some international supervision, much like the mandate system under the League of Nations that was adopted for Palestine in 1922.

In September 1918, Leonard Woolf outlined the elements he wanted to see in the Labour Party's policy on Africa, of which the most significant points were: ownership of land by natives to be safeguarded; public revenue of each colony to be devoted to the colony's native inhabitants; abolition of forced labour and the control of European capital in the interest of natives.[2] Labour's Africa specialists, such as Buxton, Woolf, Morel and Leys, saw a benign form of colonialism in British West Africa, where the economy, they claimed, was based on independent peasant producers. 'The model to follow', wrote Buxton, 'is that of the British possession on the West Coast of Africa, where the Government has treated the land as in fact the property of the native communities, has refused to alienate land to the Europeans, and has encouraged the African to make the most economic use possible of his own land'.[3] Labour's colonial experts contrasted this with Kenya where, they alleged, European enterprises were forcing the Africans into waged labour, dissolving traditional communities and undermining the power of the chiefs. In a 1924 memorandum, devoted mainly to Kenya, Morel advocated 'absolute security of land' and 'freedom for native labour' as the main preconditions for successful administration in Africa.[4]

The most comprehensive critique of settler colonialism in Kenya, in this period, came from Norman Leys, who also served on the Labour Party's Advisory Committee on Imperial Questions. The Committee formulated policy papers for discussion by the Party's National Executive Committee. In several memoranda and in two books on Kenya, Leys argued for increasing African political and economic rights. He noted that, between 1900 and 1920, the colonial authorities had appropriated more than half of the first-class land in Kenya for about 1,300 European farmers, while confining the country's three million Africans to reserves on land representing one-eighth of the colony. A European government, he claimed, 'with the rights and duties of a protector' had assumed 'the ownership of the land to give it away or to sell to its friends and countrymen'.[5] The most fertile part of the country, the so-called White Highlands, thereby passed into the exclusive ownership of European farmers. In contrast, the Kikuyu, who were pushed off some of this land into the reserves, could barely produce enough to feed themselves, while those that stayed in the White Highlands, as squatters, were compelled to work for the European farms. The 1918 Resident Native and Squatters Ordinance, Leys noted, ensured that the squatters' status was no higher than that of wage-labourers: 'they must do a minimum of 180 days' paid work in each year for the owner'.[6]

He argued that every aspect of the colonial system was geared to maintain an iniquitous land ownership system and served the European settlers at the expense of the Africans. Direct and indirect taxes fell most heavily on the poorest; the railway lines between the interior and the ports avoided the densely populated areas in order to serve mainly the European farms; the freight charges operated to make native producers subsidize the white farmers; Africans were forbidden to grow coffee and they were forced to provide six days' unpaid labour every three months for public works.

Leys called for the landless, Kenyan Africans to be given land in the central highlands. 'They must be given free grants of Crown land of the best quality. No right could be more absolute than their right to that. The land they lost by its alienation to Europeans was land of the best quality, since Europeans wanted no other sort, and nothing less must be restored to them.'[7] He stopped short, however, of demanding that the land of white farmers be taken back and redistributed among the poor and landless. His emphasis was on inaugurating a system in which Africans had equal status in law to Europeans, which he believed would assure them access to unused land in the White Highlands. The main political change he wanted was a common voters' roll, though he envisaged the vote only for the educated African.

Leys hoped for radical changes in Kenya with the coming to power in 1929 of Ramsay MacDonald's Labour government. The government's White Paper on Kenya, formulated by Lord Passfield (the former Sidney Webb), claimed to give effect to the policy of native paramountcy. It therefore rejected an in-built majority for elected European members on the Legislative Council and proposed that the colony should evolve towards a common electoral roll. The White Paper also proposed phasing out forced labour and providing protection to tribal lands against further encroachment. In the face of the settlers' determined opposition, however, Passfield abandoned plans to legislate. Leys later bitterly remarked: 'The Labour government of 1929–1931 left no mark on Colonial policy'.[8]

The NEC's policy on colonies, submitted to the 1933 party conference, counter-posed the policy of encouraging the native use of land, which it called 'the African policy', with that of encouraging syndicates or planters to use hired or forced native labour and confining the Native population to 'reserves'. It called this second orientation the 'Capitalist policy', and condemned it for leading to 'detribalisation': 'It does not aim at the creation of a self-respecting race of African producers secure in their possessions of the land, but at the evolution of a race of servile labourers divorced from the land'.[9] Detribalisation was not seen by all Labour colonial experts as something to be prevented. For example, Leys believed it to be inevitable though, apparently, it did not occur to him that the resulting African proletariat could play a political role.

The lingering hope in humanitarian circles that African society could be maintained on the basis of small peasant producers or communal ownership meant that industrial development was given only the most cursory mention before the Second World War. The Labour Party saw the rural sector as providing the solution to the growing number of landless and impoverished urban dwellers though, apart from the formation of cooperatives, it had precious few ideas about how that sector might be encouraged to develop.

In the inter-war years, British government funds for any kind of economic development in the colonies were meagre and directed, mainly, at aiding the extraction of raw materials. In the early 1920s, 90 per cent of the funds went to railway construction, nearly all in East and Central Africa.[10] The first serious attempt at a colonial development policy was initiated by the Conservatives in 1929 and then taken over by the MacDonald government in the form of the 1929 Colonial Development Act. It made available a modest £1 million per year and was inspired principally by the unemployment crisis, not by concern for colonial welfare. Even then it provoked some trade union hostility. At the TUC Conference in 1930, Bevin declared: 'I sit on a Colonial Development Committee under an Act passed by the Labour Government and I see the expenditure of millions of pounds going on for development of areas where native races have not yet begun to industrialise. You talk about the coal trade. Ought there not to be some control against the development of coal in Tanganyika and East Africa, which might come into competition with your coal here at a time when the world does not want it?'[11] A combination of such fears and the attachment to trusteeship as a way to protect the colonial peasantry from the forces of capitalism meant that, though, the Labour Party was committed to reform rather than to dismantling the Empire it lacked specific proposals on how the colonial economies might be reformed. In 1938, Creech Jones, an up-and-coming expert on colonial matters in the Party, wrote to Leys: 'I agree with you that the Party ought to have a programme for immediate action. So far we have relied on vagueness of expression which has not brought too great a credit on the Party when Labour has had the opportunity of getting something done.'[12]

Wartime policy shift

During the war years a significant shift took place in Labour's thinking on the colonies. The idea of Africa being preserved as a society of independent peasant producers was abandoned. Creech Jones called for the colonial state to lead the transformation of Britain's tropical colonies: 'There must be a big drive in social services, in education and in economic development. We must also associate the Africans in the administration of local government. We should nationalise the mineral resources of these areas. We should redistribute the land and there should be planned development of smaller industries.'[13] The 1943 statement on colonies by the Advisory Committee on Imperial Questions pointed to Africa embracing industrial development. It declared: 'the impact of the European industrial system [on African colonies] has already begun and must be considered as an important element in their future economic development...nothing can prevent the African from being drawn further and further into the European industrial system'. It then went on to speak of the need for the 'development of effective Trade Unions'.[14] Similarly, the Fabian Colonial Bureau argued, in 1942, that industry must be developed in the colonies. 'Why should Nigeria' asked Rita Hinden, 'send its oil seeds to Britain to be manufactured into soap?'[15]

Much of Labour's thinking over colonial issues in this period came from the Fabian Colonial Bureau, in which Hinden and Creech Jones were the driving force. In October 1943, Hinden presented a policy paper on Kenya. 'Since the outbreak of the war', she observed, 'the settlers have been entrenching themselves still more firmly....Their representatives dominate the new boards and Committees set up to mobilise the country in the war effort. Through this domination they have been able to introduce legislation, guaranteeing very high prices for their crops; and where, as in the case of maize, the crop happens to be produced by Africans as well, the guaranteed very high prices have been confined to the Europeans only'. She went on to argue that it was not 'practical politics' to liquidate the white farming community but nor could its plans for further settlement and the preservations of its existing privileges be supported: 'there must be no new European settlement schemes financed by public funds either British or local—and no more encouragement given to further European settlement'. Hinden accepted that the Europeans had contributed to the development of East Africa but added that 'it had been at a heavy cost to the African community' and questioned whether this contribution 'could be considered indispensable'.[16]

A couple of months later, Creech Jones reiterated several of these points, in the House of Commons. He welcomed the government's move to limit forced labour to sisal production and expressed the hope that in that sector, too, this 'reprehensible practice' would be abandoned. He called for a positive development policy towards the African reserves and was critical of extending European settlement, though his criticism was self-consciously cautious. He advanced the implausible argument that such an extension would be more damaging for the settler farmers than for the Africans. 'The policy of European settlement has been costly to the Colony and, most of all, costly to large numbers of the individuals who were attracted to settle in the Colony....That colonisation has been sustained by subsidising from Colonial revenues, by distorting the natural economy and by neglect of the native areas....It has been sustained also by the neglect of the vital social services and by a disparity in treatment by European and African in such matters as health and education.'[17] The following year, on his return from a visit to West Africa, Creech Jones endorsed the view put to him, he said, by Africans, that little of the huge profits made from African products found their way back to the producers. 'The complaints are well founded and socialist criticism of economic imperialism is well grounded.'[18]

Once the Labour government assumed power in 1945 and Creech Jones moved to the Colonial Office—first as junior minister and then, from October 1946, as Secretary of State—the policies pursued towards Kenya showed no trace of the 'socialist criticism of economic imperialism'. Creech Jones came round to defending the economic measures that, in opposition, he had attacked. He now supported the extension of European settlement in Kenya, on the basis of the important contribution European farmers made to the country's development[19] and justified the use of forced labour on the basis that it was necessary for improving the African farming areas. A Colonial Office circular of 1947 dispatched to African governors stated: 'there can be no question as to the necessity of ensuring that proper methods of cultivation are adopted and that the soil is conserved, and if this can only be achieved by the use of compulsory powers, then the native administration will have to take such powers'.[20] It was this preoccupation with increasing production in the colonies that was the immediate cause for Creech Jones's abandonment of the policies he had espoused. Labour's plans for rebuilding the economy after the war were hindered by shortages in certain key commodities and, still more crucially, by a shortage of dollars. In the light of these difficulties, which Labour leaders believed put their domestic reforms in peril, the colonies were subsumed into a project of increasing agricultural production by the introduction of modern farming techniques. Africa's part in this vision was spelt out by Stafford Cripps:

> Tropical Africa is already contributing much, both in physical supplies of food and raw materials and in quite substantial net earning of dollars for the sterling area pool....We must be prepared to change our own habits of colonial development and force the pace so that within the next two

to five years we can get a really marked increase of production in coal, minerals, timber, raw materials of all kinds, foodstuffs and anything else that will save dollars or will sell in the dollar market...

You will I understand be considering the question of the development of manufacturers and industries in the Colonies. Though I take the view that such development is highly desirable so long as it is not pushed too far or too quickly, yet it must be obvious that with the present world shortage of capital goods, it is not possible to contemplate much in the way of industrial development in the colonies...[21]

The drive to increase Africa's contribution to the metropolitan economy thus led the Labour Party leadership to downplay industrial development there and to abandon its opposition to forced labour, the abolishment of which had been emblematic for the humanitarian lobby of a more enlightened colonialism. For the same reason, the Labour government also turned against opening the White Highlands to African farming. Creech Jones endorsed a 25 per cent increase in the number of settlers. A memorandum by the Party's Advisory Committee noted with dismay: 'The African reserves are overcrowded, and consequently are rapidly losing such fertility as they possess. Rehabilitation of the reserves is impossible until the density of the population is reduced. The Highlands is the only land available.'[22] The Advisory Committee's disillusionment with the government's Kenya policy led its Secretary to conclude that Creech Jones's policy was indistinguishable from that of his Tory predecessors.[23] In one sphere there was, however, a difference. The preoccupation with increasing Kenya's agricultural output left intact the party's previous commitment to overhaul the institutions that operated on the local level under chiefs and headmen. The modernisation of African agriculture required new partners for the colonial state.

Changing élites

Developing African participation in local institutions was something that Woolf and others had suggested in the 1920s. It was subsequently taken up by the Fabian Colonial Bureau, which was initiated in 1940 by Creech Jones and Rita Hinden. The Bureau, which for a decade came to 'canalize virtually the entire flow of party ideas on colonial affairs',[24] argued that democratising native institutions was a necessary preparation for eventual self-government. Creech Jones's strong commitment to this project, after 1945, could be interpreted—with some justice—as an attempt to maintain Labour's reformist credentials. Yet the fact that the Colonial Office also became an enthusiastic supporter of developing local government in Africa suggests that it was more than a camouflage for the Labour government's abandonment of attempting structural changes in colonial economies. It was, in fact, a mechanism for drawing Africa's educated stratum into the task of increasing the tropic's agricultural output. As Creech Jones explained: 'the problem of increased productivity is closely connected with the development of an efficient system of local government.'[25]

Pearce, unstinting in his admiration for Creech Jones and the Colonial Office's imperial reforms, explains their determination to reform Kenya's local government in the following way:

> While Lugard centred his policy on the chiefs as the native authority and dismissed the educated élite, Cohen [Andrew Cohen was head of the Africa Division of the Colonial Office] and Creech Jones emphasised that it would be the council, and the educated African members who would control the local authority, while the power of the chiefs would steadily decline…Local government was to fulfill the function of giving politicians political experience and inculcating responsibility to a new generation of African politicians, while at the same time, by a system of indirect election, it was to exclude a premature transfer of power to a small unrepresentative group of 'ballot-box politicians'.[26]

This change of élites—through the modernisation but limited democratisation of the native institutions—was perceived as important for increasing the colonies' marketable surplus which, as mentioned above, the Labour government urgently desired. Hence, at the same time, state-promoted development initiatives were greatly expanded. Treasury funds under the 1940 Development and Welfare Act were increased—though tied mainly to provision of social services—and, in 1947, the Colonial Development Corporation and the Overseas Food Corporation were set up, involving the British government directly for the first time in managing production in the colonies.

The drive to increase productivity in the African reserves of Kenya required, however, if anything, a still more autocratic local state. A growing army of technical experts was recruited to guide and exert pressure on the peasantry. The Colonial Office recognised the economic significance of the educated and westernised élite and the importance of co-opting it. Local government was advocated as political training that would prepare this élite for self-government. Yet neither the Colonial Office mandarins, nor Creech Jones, believed that Africa was anywhere near attaining self-government and the involvement of the educated stratum in local administration had the more immediate purpose of confining nationalist politicians to the local level. The Fabian Colonial Bureau and the Colonial Office, whose basic outlook converged after the war, wanted local government only as an instrument of agricultural modernisation. Creech Jones feared that the politicisation of educated Africans 'may result in the creation of a class of professional African politicians absorbed in the activities of the centre and out of direct touch with the people themselves'.[27] The obvious solution to this danger was universal suffrage, which would have made the political élite accountable, at least to some degree, to the people. The dilemma for the post-war imperial reformers was, however, that they wanted the Western-educated Africans to play a part in economic development but not in political mobilisation. An 'emotional nationalism', Creech Jones warned, 'will make the work of the colonial state (however broadly based) very difficult'.[28] The roles he and the Colonial Office wanted for educated Africans were as experts and administrators on development committees and marketing boards, not as tribunes for popular demands. A post-war vocabulary was introduced to provide the ideological underpinning for introducing this new stratum in place of the more traditional agents of indirect rule. This limited political change was designated as part of the post-war relation between Britain and her colonies: 'partnership' replaced 'trusteeship' as the key term in a discourse that was adopted by both Labour and Conservatives.

There was a feeling in the Labour Party that behind these cosmetic changes Labour's period in office had left it with no distinctive policies. The Commonwealth Sub-Committee which, at the end of 1949, had absorbed the Advisory Committee on Imperial Questions, observed a year later: 'No clear statement of Labour party policy concerning the Colonies has been made since the war...There is a great deal of uneasiness today and many responsible persons and journals have called for redefinition and restatement of British Colonial policy.'[29] Arthur Lewis, a Jamaican-born academic on the left of the Party, was scornful of the change of terminology. Referring to Kenya, he observed: 'The period of trusteeship was used to settle the trustee's sons upon the property and to give them powers of administration. That is how trusteeship became partnership....By partnership they mean a society in which all Europeans are always at the top'.[30]

A few months after Lewis's article appeared, the British state was confronted with the Mau Mau rebellion, which posed a serious threat to Kenya's Europeans remaining 'at the top'. By this time Labour was in opposition. The public discussion that ensued took place largely within the terms set by the debate between the Tories and Labour. In this debate, Kenya functioned largely as a synonym for 'the African'. Although both parties wanted

Mau Mau militarily defeated, Labour proved more prepared to accept political reforms that might accommodate the African nationalist élite. Creech Jones had rightly claimed a few years earlier: 'Surprisingly to some, but none the less significantly, it is the Labour Party which is becoming the real Empire Party, while the Tories hobble along in the rear shackled by the slogans of yesterday, which mean little or nothing in the new Commonwealth of today'.[31]

The first Parliamentary debate on Mau Mau was in November 1952. The Conservative government's position was put by Oliver Lyttelton, the Colonial Secretary. 'Mau Mau,' he declared, 'is not the child of economic pressure...Let us be clear on this point: that Mau Mau is a secret society and feeds not upon economic discontent, but is something far more sinister. It is the enemy of the law abiding African. It is anti-Christ and it feeds not upon economic discontent but upon perverted nationalism and on a sort of nostalgia for barbarism.'[32] In his memoirs some ten years later, he still saw Mau Mau as the incarnation of evil: 'I can recall no instance when I have felt the forces of evil to be so near or so strong. As I wrote memoranda or instructions, I would suddenly see a shadow fall across the page—the horned shadow of the devil himself'.[33] *Daily Mail* reports of the rebellion used similar images. Under the title 'Educated Men Organising the Pagan Terrorists', its Nairobi correspondent wrote:

> Even the meaning of the words Mau Mau is a mystery....A theory which is possibly nearest the truth is that the words are a cover name for 'man-eaters', the man-eater being a mythical figure in Kikuyu folk-lore who devours human flesh....Happily the Mau Mau society is confined to the Kikuyu tribe....They are regarded as of inferior physique and unfit for heavy labour but they are credited with finesse in circumventing obstacles they are unable to surmount....The Kikuyu clearly covets the land of his European neighbours which is prospering under intensive farming methods. His envy, however, is more that of the inefficient for the efficient than that of the 'have nots' for the 'haves'.[34]

This was the language of crude Social Darwinism, widely held in both the Tory party and among Kenya's European settlers. It served to legitimise the policy of depriving the Kenyan Africans of both land and political power and to deny any political significance to the rebellion. In the *Daily Telegraph*, Elspeth Huxley, who was brought up in Kenya and was considered an East African expert, speculated that colonial rule had imposed a veneer of civilisation on Kenya which was incompatible with the African's nature: 'the average African is immured in a grey world of peasantry and clerkhood, regulated by Civil Servants and almost wholly devoid of spectacles and orgies. No wonder he suffers from boredom and impatience and quickly joins the Mau Mau in the hope of a little excitement.'[35]

From the Labour press, the first report on Mau Mau was in the form of a loose summary in the *Daily Herald* of Lyttelton's speech in the Commons. Its tone was light hearted and evoked an image of Africa in the style of Rider Haggard. Under the title: 'Dancing Banned So Tribes Turn to Terror' it reported: 'Suppression of tribal dances by missionaries and compulsion to pay for wives in money instead of cattle, were two reasons given in the Commons last night for the outbreak of terrorism by the Mau Mau secret society in Kenya'.[36] The report was a highly selective summary of Lyttelton's speech but, more significantly, since it suggested no other interpretation, the reader was invited to take the reported speech at face value. This initial response was not out of line with the Attlee governments' legacy: their defence of European farming in Kenya as a bastion of modern farming in the midst of African backwardness had eclipsed the Labour Party's tradition of opposition to the colour bar and to the economics of settler colonialism. Out of government, the Labour leadership, however, reverted to a more radical position. In July 1952, it again called for unused land in the White Highlands to be made available to African farmers. Yet, even then, it considered the position of European farming inviolate. In a Parliamentary motion supported by 150 Labour MPs, it argued that the government should develop African agriculture through the spread of modern techniques and the provision of credit, 'rather than to continue sterile controversies about tribal claims to land at present reserved for European settlement'.[37] The redistribution of European land to Africans was consequently placed outside the realm of mainstream political debate in Britain, and remained so even after it became evident that this was at the core of Mau Mau's demands.

Labour MPs categorically condemned Mau Mau. There was in this respect no difference between the two main parties. The report of an all-party delegation to Kenya summarised the bi-partisan approach. It stated: 'Mau Mau intentionally and deliberately seeks to lead the Africans and the Kikuyu back to the bush and savagery, not forward into progress.'[38] The cause of Mau Mau was attributed by Labour to socio-economic factors, and by the Tories to the African personality. There was, nevertheless, the odd Labour voice that overlapped with the Tory discourse. George Wigg, who was to take an active part in discussions over Kenya, declared: 'Those of us who have any acquaintance with Africa know that witchcraft is only just below the surface there....It may be called Mau Mau today, but tomorrow it may be called Go Go or Ba Ba. It may be out of sight of the District Commissioner and the police but the secret society with its witchcraft and revolting practices is there all the time. It is endemic, it is part of the African way of life.'[39] The party leadership, however, insisted that the causes of the Mau Mau rebellion lay in the socio-economic conditions of the Kikuyu, and the *Daily Herald* after its first equivocal report promoted this position with frequent editorials. Ultimately, though, Labour's analysis was not radically different from that of the Conservatives. It merely tended to substitute for the claim that Kikuyu poverty was rooted in the innate qualities of the African the idea that it was rooted in the backwardness of African culture. As Cooper has noted, this enabled the same strictures to be made about culture that in the post-war period had become increasing unacceptable to make about 'race'.[40]

A State of Emergency was declared in Kenya in October 1952. The British objective in the first phase of the war was to secure the central Highlands. About 100,000 African workers from the estates and towns of this region were repatriated to the reserves, adding pressure on the resources there and causing serious food shortages. Three brigades of British soldiers and 20,000 police waged a war that lasted until 1956, when Mau Mau as a military force was defeated. 11,500 so-called terrorists, about 2000 African civilians and 95 Europeans were killed. 'By the end of 1954, 18,069 Kikuyu, Embu and Meru were in prison after conviction for various "Mau Mau" offences, while 49,289 others were detained in detention camps without trial.'[41] Mau Mau fighters were predominantly rural Kikuyu. Their leadership, based mainly in the Nairobi slums, had little connection with the established political groups, though several Kenyan African National Union leaders, including Jomo Kenyatta, were imprisoned on suspicion of leading the rebellion.

Towards political reform

In Parliament, James Griffiths, putting the Labour leadership's case, and Fenner Brockway, from the left of the party, a long-time champion of anti-colonial causes, emphasised that land hunger was Mau Mau's immediate cause. The party called for 'a policy which will permit Africans, and in particular African cooperatives to own land in the highlands'.[42] Over the following years, Labour leaders became increasingly critical of what they considered as excessive reliance by the Government on military repression to deal with Mau Mau. Their criticism appeared to uphold the tradition of anti-colonialism for which there was some pressure from the left of the party and from the ranks. Before the end of 1952, two constituency parties had sent a resolution to the NEC demanding the 'transfer of wealth to the peoples of Kenya and support in their struggles' and a further twenty-five constituency parties supported a resolution condemning the government's policy of collective punishment and demanding 'a more constructive policy'.[43]

The Labour leadership concentrated on two aspects of the government's effort to defeat Mau Mau. First, it argued that it failed to address the underlying causes. Griffiths demanded action on the land problem and for 'the progressive elimination of the colour bar, co-operative farming and the raising of wage standards, extension of free education, the creation of new industries and provision of housing, and the democratisation of local government.'[44] Second, it attacked the government's repression of what Labour called 'the responsible African leaders', who were necessary, it argued, if the Kikuyu were to be won away from Mau Mau to an alternative leadership. Labour disagreed, therefore, with the means which the Conservative government employed to defeat Mau Mau rather than with its overall political objectives. During the war years, Creech Jones had discussed the European farming sector in terms of its detrimental impact on the African population, pointing to the pressure of land and to the diversion of resources, but once ensconced, as minister, in the Colonial Office and pursuing the policy of modernising African agriculture, he discussed the two sectors as self-contained entities. He abandoned Leys' and Woolf's pre-war view that the problems of African agriculture resulted from colonialism—a view that had been widely accepted in the party, including by Creech Jones—suggesting, instead, that they were problems inherent to Africa. In 1950, in a speech designed to defend the Labour government's colonial policies, Creech Jones argued: 'It is beside the mark to make capitalism a convenient scapegoat for what is wrong in the colonial territories. In the vast and dark continent of Africa it is tribal and primitive people, enchained by ignorance and custom and superstition whom we are seeking to advance.'[45] His analysis of the causes of Mau Mau rebellion was in the same vein. When asked in a radio discussion what he thought of the claim that the whites held the best land in Kenya, he replied: 'It is not the case, I think. Some of the very best land is held by Africans. It is a question of good husbandry; the fact that the Government are not able to give all the assistance they would like....You have some of the best land enjoyed by Africans. The European land alongside looks marvelously good, and that of the African land, because of neglect, looks in a very, very bad state indeed, right down to the rock.'[46]

The rapidly escalating violence in Kenya did not cause the party to reflect on whether the policy it had pursued there, when in government, may have been partly responsible. The party leadership had moved so far from its colonial experts' pre-war, humanitarian critique of settler colonialism, it had imbibed, so deeply, the view that the state of African farming was primarily the result of backward techniques and culture, that the grievances generated by socio-economic structure escaped its attention. In 1930, Leys had warned: 'Remember that African grievances are pent up....We are not far off an explosion....Granted that trouble will start among the Kikuyu, no one can say, once started how it will spread.'[47] A decade later he again noted: 'No European can judge how near people's patience in East Africa is to breaking point.'[48]

Leys, by his humanitarian and democratic criteria, had a better measure of the African peasantry's situation, than did the Fabian-inspired, post-war Labour leadership, even when the latter faced a full-scale, rural rebellion. In 1953, after a visit to Kenya, George Brown told a meeting of the Overseas League:

> the Africans have a vast amount of land if they were only as good as the Europeans at handling it...I discovered that it was not true at all that all the fertile land in Africa is in the hands of the whites...I saw land every bit as fertile, in some cases more fertile than the land in the White Highlands. Therefore, it is not true that the whites have stolen all the best land in Africa. Of course there is still far more land unalienated in Kenya. I think the real problem is to fetch some of that land into cultivation....One final thing, if you gave the whole of the White Highlands to the Africans it would, if I may use the phrase, be rather like giving a gooseberry to an elephant.[49]

In opposition, as in government, Labour saw the European farmers as the cornerstone of the Kenyan economy and, therefore, advocated developing African agriculture without challenging their economic dominance.

It was on the level of political reform that Labour was more open to a new approach. In this respect, the party leadership moved beyond Leys, though by updating rather than abandoning his paternalism. He had argued that when revolt came in East Africa 'it will be a far ghastlier business than elsewhere' because among Africans there were 'no educated, high minded men like De Valera or Nehru. Trouble when it comes will, we may be sure, be directed by men so ignorant, so venal, so irresponsible, that no Governor will have any course alternative to crushing it.'[50] Since the war, however, as a result of Labour's acceptance that African societies needed to evolve, gradually, towards self-government and that the educated stratum had to be trained for that eventuality, the party was, ideologically, more predisposed than the Conservatives to try to incorporate Kenya's nationalist politicians into the political system.

Whereas the Conservatives in the mid-1950s still believed that the colonial state's appointed chiefs and headmen could contain the traditional African society and thereby ensure the unhindered development of the European farming sector, Labour looked to the native educated élite, that occupied the subaltern ranks in the colonial state, to modernise the African sector itself. Their fear and mistrust of the African masses were no less pronounced than that of the Conservatives. There was 'no going back to the jungle' declared James Griffiths, who succeeded Creech Jones as Labour's shadow minister on colonial affairs: 'One day I went to Makarere College and spoke to some African students. It was like speaking to university students anywhere else....Two days afterwards I was in Nyanza Province and saw dances in the bush. In 24 hours we moved thousands of years and saw the two types of Africans. There are Africans in the bush, but there are also Africans in the study room.'[51] Labour had no doubts that it was the African of the study room who should provide the 'alternative leadership'. It championed the cause of this group in opposition to the 'rootless proletariat' and the 'bush savage', who held out the danger of causing Africa to revert to barbarism.

These racist stereotypes served to obscure from the British public and labour movement the economic realties in the African reserves and the peasantry's demand for land, which had been the driving force behind the Mau Mau rebellion. It also left untouched the increasingly dominant role, in the Kenyan economy, of the large foreign corporations. The Labour leadership was only too eager to confer legitimacy on the moderate nationalist leadership with whom the Conservative government negotiated the terms of a land settlement, majority rule and independence. The land settlement was the key to the new political and economic order. In March 1961, the British government announced a scheme to divide up 180,000 acres of the White Highlands into mainly 50-acre farm units. From the Labour Party in Parliament this brought the criticism that the government was seeking to create an African middle class. 'Perhaps they feel that, in due course, they will become back-bencher African baronets in a future Conservative Kenyan legislature'.[52] But Labour's own policy of cultivating the educated élite to cooperate with the colonial state did not permit a radically different land settlement.

In response to nationalist pressure, the British government modified its initial scheme, in 1962, and decided to make available a million acres for the settlement of 75,000 families, of which about 30,000 were to be landless families. The landless had to purchase their land by loans from Britain and the World Bank, the repayment of which locked them into the prevailing system of production and marketing. Labour welcomed the scheme's introduction. It conformed to its own conception of handing over land in the White Highlands to 'farmers who are able and willing to abide by good farming regulations'.[53] Labour could not have anticipated the onerous debt burden that was imposed on the peasant cultivators who took up loans to buy land under the settlement scheme, nor could it have influenced the terms of the land settlement even if it had opposed them—the significance of its position lay elsewhere. By rejecting the more left-wing nationalist demand that the European owned land should be distributed free to the poor peasantry and the landless, it consolidated the party's vision of decolonisation within the narrow limits of handing over the colonial state to the indigenous élite. Labour was prepared to see new trustees for Africans, not the emergence of a different type of politics and economic structure.

The restructuring in the White Highlands formed the key element of the agreement with Britain that led to Kenya's political élite acceding to independence, in 1963. By the early 1970s, 40 per cent of white farms were sold on a loan-tied basis, opening the way for settling 500,000 Africans. The remaining 60 per cent 'were largely transferred intact to wealthy Africans'.[54] The basis of Kenya's 'open economy' was put in place.

Notes

1. *The Times*, 13 November 1952. The Mau Mau rebellion broke out in 1952 and was finally suppressed by the British army in 1956. Most Mau Mau fighters came from the Kikuyu, the ethnic group which had been most affected by European land appropriation and capitalist development. The rebels aimed to recover land from the European settlers. Their ideology drew on ideas common to many anti-colonial struggles as well as on folkloric constructions of the Kikuyu's past.
2. L.S. Woolf, 'Colonies', Labour Party Advisory Committee on Imperial Questions (henceforth LPACImp.Q) file 1918–1920, Labour Party Archives, National Museum of Labour History, Manchester (henceforth NMLH).
3. C.R. Buxton, LPACImp.Q. Memo. no. 26, c.1925.
4. E.D. Morel, LPACImp.Q. Memo. no. 2, April 1924.
5. Norman Leys, *A Last Chance in Kenya* (London, 1931), p.143.
6. Leys, *Last Chance*, p.56.
7. Leys, *Last Chance*, p.64.
8. Norman Leys, LPACImp.Q. Memo. no. 205, February 1939.

9. 'The Colonies', National Executive Committee submission to 1933 Labour Party conference.
10. Michael Havinden and David Meredith, *Colonialism and Development. Britain and its tropical colonies* (London, 1993), p.140.
11. P.S. Gupta, *Imperialism and the British Labour Movement, 1914–1964* (London, 1975), p.154.
12. Creech Jones to Leys, 10 February 1939 in Arthur Creech Jones papers, Rhodes House, Oxford box 14, file 1.
13. Richard Pearce, *The Turning Point in Africa. British colonial policy, 1938–1948* (London, 1982), p.102.
14. *The Colonies* (London: Labour Party Advisory Committee on Imperial Questions, 1943).
15. Rita Hinden et al., *Freedom For Colonial Peoples* (London: Peace Aims pamphlet, 1942).
16. LPACImp.Q. Memo. No.263, October 1943.
17. House of Commons *Debates*, vol. 395, col. 1906, 17 December 1943.
18. *Left News*, August 1944.
19. House of Commons *Debates*, vol. 420, col. 130, 7 March 1946.
20. Colonial Office circular dispatch to African governors, 22 February 1947, cited in Richard Hyam, *The Labour Government and the End of Empire*, vol. 2 (London, 1992).
21. Quoted in Rita Hinden, *Commonsense and Colonial Development* (London: Fabian Colonial Bureau, 1949).
22. LPACImp.Q. Memo. No. 296B, April 1946.
23. LPACImp.Q. minutes, 4 June, 1947
24. David Goldsworthy, *Colonial Issues in British Politics* (Oxford, 1971), p.123.
25. Pearce, *Turning Point*, p.159.
26. Pearce, *Turning Point*, p.158.
27. Creech Jones to Governors of the African Territories, Letter, 25 February 1947, Creech Jones papers, box 15, file 3.
28. *Tribune*, 11 August 1950.
29. 'Need for a new policy statement on colonial affairs', Labour Party Commonwealth Sub-Committee, n.d. probably January 1951, LP/CSC/50/21, NMLH.
30. *New Statesman*, 17 July 1952.
31. *Tribune*, 11 February 1949.
32. House of Commons *Debates*, vol. 507, col. 474, 7 November 1952.
33. Cited in Bruce Berman, *Control and Crisis in Colonial Kenya* (London, 1996) p.355.
34. *Daily Mail*, 16 October 1952.
35. *Daily Telegraph*, 17 September 1952.
36. *Daily Herald*, 17 October 1952.
37. Labour Party Commonwealth Sub-Committee, 28 May 1952, LP/CSC.52/40.
38. *Report to the Secretary of State for Colonies by the Parliamentary Delegation to Kenya*, Cmd. 9081, 1954, p.4.

39. House of Commons *Debates*, vol. 507, col. 505, 17 July 1952.
40. Frederick Cooper, *Decolonization and African Society. The land question in French and British Africa* (Cambridge, 1996), p.17.
41. Berman, *Control and Crisis*, p.351.
42. House of Commons *Debates*, vol. 505, col. 2350, 17 July 1952.
43. 'Analysis of resolutions on colonial policy received from November 1952-January 1953', Labour Party Commonwealth Sub-Committee, LP/CSC.52/32.
44. House of Commons *Debates*, vol. 509, col. 1212, 16 December 1952.
45. A. Creech Jones, Labour Party and Fabian Colonial Bureau conference, 23 September 1950, Creech Jones papers, box 4, file 4.
46. *East Africa and Rhodesia*, 23 April 1953.
47. LPACImp.Q. Memo. no. 82, November 1930.
48. LPACImp.Q. Memo. no. 217, February 1940.
49. George Brown and Charles Hobson, *Kenya Impressions* (London, 1953).
50. LPACImp.Q. Memo. no. 217, February 1940.
51. House of Commons *Debates*, vol. 507, col. 480, 7 November 1952.
52. House of Commons *Debates*, vol. 637, col. 1605, 30 March 1961.
53. 'Memorandum submitted by the Fabian Colonial Bureau to Royal Commission on Land and Population in East Africa', Creech Jones papers, box 21, file 3.
54. Berman, *Control and Crisis*, p.412.

The 'Strike of 400,000' and the Organisation of Workers in São Paulo, Brazil, 1957

Paulo Fontes

The period of the government of President Juscelino Kubitscheck (1956–1961) is considered to be one of the most important in twentieth-century Brazilian history. It has been seen as the zenith of the national development model and as an era of political stability and economic prosperity. The period has been associated with the optimistic image of Brazil as the 'country of the future'. The Brazilian victory in the Football World Cup in 1958 and the international repercussions of cultural events such as Bossa Nova and Cinema Novo helped to build the idea of a Brazilian 'golden age', which is associated with Kubitscheck's government. The slogan '50 years of development in 5 years', the setting up of the automobile industry as well as the building of the new federal capital, Brasilia, still remain as symbols of that period.

An important feature of this historical representation is the concealment of the social struggles that were taking place at that time. From this perspective, the assumption is that class conflict and political tensions were characteristics either of the previous period, the so-called 'Vargas era', or of the 1960s, with the administration of João Goulart, the military coup and the leftwing guerrillas. Thus, from this viewpoint, Kubitscheck's government is seen as an oasis of social stability.[1]

However, the period of the Kubitscheck government did see several important social struggles. In the rural areas, the rising of the peasant movement (the *Ligas Camponesas*) put the debate about land reform on the political agenda. In the major cities and in the industrialised regions, the workers campaigned for their rights and for a better standard of living, and organised themselves into militant trade unions. The working class was not a passive element during the 'golden age'. It participated influentially in the social, economic and political life of the country.

The 'Strike of 400,000', as it became known, took place in São Paulo in October, 1957. This episode is fundamental to our understanding of the intricate social and political relationships during those years. It was considered at the time to be 'the biggest strike that has ever taken place in this country'.[2] The stoppage involved different trade unions in São Paulo and nearby cities, such as Santo André, Jundiaí and Sorocaba. The 'Strike of 400,000' is considered by most of the literature of that period as a typical strike of the 'populist era'. For many authors, this stoppage was merely an action of a bureaucratic union movement. According to them, its leadership was politically aware, while the proletariat, on the other hand, had little or no class consciousness, owing to its rural origin. The trade unions are not seen as having any organisation in the workplace and the strikes are considered to be merely the result of picket actions. The pickets are the 'proof' of a movement organised from the top down (in the trade unions) and from the outside to the inside (in the factories).[3]

This article critically examines this predominant view of the 'Strike of 400,000' specifically, and the workers movement of that period in general. It emphasises the importance of the workers' action and attempts to demonstrate how they were active in the strike as well as in their forms of participation and organisation. It also underlines the common experience of those workers in their everyday life within the factories and in their neighbourhoods. Beyond huge differences in terms of ethnicity, gender, skill, politics, etc., the 'Strike of 400,000' was a fundamental moment of class formation and it is essential to an understanding of that important period of Brazilian history.

The struggle against inflation

Growing dissatisfaction with the inflationary effects of the government's economic policies was visible among the workers in 1957. Many protests and demonstrations against the rising cost of living took place during that year. Wages bore the brunt of this process. The increase in labour productivity was not followed by increases in remuneration, resulting in a lower standard of living.[4]

Thus, the unions sought to link the struggle for better wages with price controls, especially the price of essential goods. Speeches of the PUI (Unions Unity Pact)[5] leaders, for instance, often stressed the gap between workers' wages and inflation. They tried to connect it with workplace conditions and with the employers' profits:

> Although the bosses seek to demonstrate that they cannot improve wages, the industry situation is good.... The workers' situation is becoming worse

and worse because of inflation and the consequent decrease in real wages. Exploitation within the factories rises, the rhythm of the assembly lines intensifies, our rights are constantly ignored, while bread on the workers' table always diminishes.[6]

This kind of speech corresponded very closely to the workers' feelings and anxieties. A pickets' leader said that the most successful argument to convince the workers to join the strike was to make 'a parallel between the employers' profits and the squalid workers' salaries'. A textile worker, some days before the strike, complained that his boss 'has earned $54 million, while my family is starving'.[7]

The pressure for wage increases was growing. Strikes were breaking out in several factories and, through the PUI, the main unions were seeking to unite the struggle into one joint campaign. At the beginning of October, the metalworkers', textile workers', glass workers', graphics and paper workers' unions decided to join forces in order to negotiate with the employers' federation (FIESP). They demanded a 45 per cent general increase in wages and measures against inflation.

The employers, however, claiming that their economic situation was bad, refused to negotiate any increase in wages. The inflexibility of the bosses exacerbated the leaders' and those workers' dissatisfaction. According to a report about the strike, written by the North American consulate in São Paulo, the 'employers' intransigence' was listed as one of the main causes of the movement.[8]

The unions intensified the mobilisation and organisation for a likely strike. Assemblies, outdoor meetings and parades were held, creating a growing atmosphere of mobilisation. Textile union leaders, for instance, reported that 'more than 100 factories were visited, reaching around 300,000 workers, who were watching the struggle against inflation with great enthusiasm'.[9]

On 15 October 1957, the strike began with great support from the workers. Nearly 80 per cent of those workers, whose unions were involved in the movement, joined it. Many pickets, some of them with thousands of workers in their lines, guaranteed the efficiency of the strike. On its second day, the strike continued even more strongly. The stoppage reached almost 100 per cent. Taking advantage of the strike, the general population manifested its dissatisfaction and took to the streets. There were violent scenes and nearly 50 people were injured as a result of clashes between strikers and security guards in some factories. Some factories were even wrecked.

The employers blamed the absence of policing and the conduct of Jânio Quadros,[10] the Governor of São Paulo state, as the main causes of the 'alarming proportions' of the strike. Quadros particularly irritated the employers when he declared that 'the government is not a praetorian guard of economic power'.[11] Businessmen debated openly whether they should ask for federal and military intervention in the state. Antonio Devisate, president of FIESP, had several meetings with Juscelino Kubitschek demanding concrete measures against the strike.

Jânio Quadros, frightened by these threats, promised to police the streets and to repress the strike. Thus, on the third day of the strike, thousands of policemen started to watch the factories and the streets. Despite this police presence, the strike continued strongly and even began to spread to other cities. In practice, the workers were weakening the employers' argument that the strike had only taken place because of the absence of police.

Since all attempts at negotiation between employers and workers had failed, on the tenth day of the movement, the dispute was arbitrated by the TRT (Labour Regional Court). The court decreed a 25 per cent wage rise to all workers involved. Although the result was less than the 45 per cent initially demanded, it was much more than the employers were willing to give and the workers' and unions' leaderships celebrated the judgement as a great victory of the strike.

Sympathy and understanding

There was a great deal of political interest surrounding the strike. The stoppage took place in a period of intense electoral contests and several political parties competed in search of workers' votes. In March of that year, the Jânio Quadros candidate had lost the election for the City Council of São Paulo. For Quadros it was essential to recover his popularity because of the next state election that would take place in 1958, and the presidential election in 1960. As North American observers pointed out, the strike was a chance:

> to maintain and strengthen his following in the labor ranks....From conversations with the man in the street it is clear that the public understands that the Governor cannot afford to turn his back to the potential labor backing, reds and all. No matter how distasteful to him personally this might have been, the Governor had to go along with the strike.[13]

At the same time Quadros tried to retain his influence in the trade unions of São Paulo. Even during the most difficult and tense moments of the strike, he always tried to keep in touch with the unionists. He also made efforts to maintain a direct relationship with ordinary workers. The state government provided foodstuffs, medicines and other resources for the strikers. Despite the fact that Jânio Quadros, under the pressure of employers and the federal government, ordered the police to repress the movement, his image as a governor sympathetic to the strike and as an ally to the workers seems to have remained strong among the population. This image might have helped the victory of his candidate in the state election, and Quadros himself in his triumph in the presidential election of 1960.

It was not only Jânio Quadros, however, who tried to appear as a 'friend' of the workers. Adhemar de Barros, Mayor of São Paulo and another famous example of a populist politician during the 1940s and 1950s, declared his help for the strike and provided some resources for the movement. Councillors and politicians of all parties, indeed even rightwingers, declared support for the strike, and many of them took part in some pickets and demonstrations. The most famous case was the participation of the Vice-Governor of the state, General Porfirio da Paz, in a 'monster-picket' at Alpargatas, a big textile factory. He was strongly criticised by the employers and by the conservative press, which nicknamed him 'major picket maker'.

Although the politicians attempted to take advantage of the strike, at the same time they were also being 'used' by the workers. Luis Tenorio Lima, a communist leader of foodstuff workers, recalled how Porfirio da Paz was taken unawares in that same episode:

> We were gathering in the stadium. More than 50 thousand workers...Porfirio da Paz, as usual, went on to declare that he was very sympathetic to the strike. He was a very nice kind of guy, open minded, much too religious, but a democratic person. He was really applauded and at the end of his speech he said: 'Here I am not a General, here I am your soldier.' As soon as he said that, Dante Pelacani (graphic workers' union leader) spoke up: 'If you, General, are our soldier, the workers demand that you come together with us in a picket to stop the work at *Alpargatas*.' Porfirio had never expected anything like that, but he couldn't refuse to join the picket. Then a crowd of workers and the General went to that factory. A delegation of strikers and Porfirio da Paz went into the workplace. Who could forbid the Vice-Governor of São Paulo to enter the factory? Alpargatas opened its gates and its workers joined the strike. That's why Porfirio da Paz became so famous.[14]

During the strike, the main political parties supported or, at least, did not oppose the workers' movement. 'Nearly all the political currents attempted to use the strike in some way to their advantage', provisionally isolating the employers and reinforcing the image of the strike as a legal and fair movement. A communist militant admitted at the beginning of the strike that there was an 'atmosphere of sympathy and understanding'.[15]

The importance of the working class in political life was a central feature of Brazilian society after the Second World War. In São Paulo, the most industrialised state, the role of urban workers was decisive in electoral contests. The businessmen sought to adapt themselves to this new political scenario. Nevertheless, as this strike represented a critical situation for the employers, they came up with heavy criticisms against 'this mob of demagogues that is encouraging the disorder among the workers of São Paulo…politicians, who are basically enemies of our country'.[16]

However, the workers, apart from being victims of the manipulation of 'demagogues', were very aware of their role in the country's political life and sought to strike in this complex scenario. Communist militants asserted that in São Paulo 'nobody can think of being the main political force standing against the proletariat'.[17] Far from being an isolated position of the communists, the consciousness of their importance in the political arena was growing among the workers. When a police captain, for instance, repressing a picket, said that 'the order is to beat the dogs up', indignant women workers[18] answered that they had 'the right to vote to "put our man at the top"', who would appoint the police chiefs. Many workers clearly expressed their awareness about the politicians' electoral interests hidden behind the help given.

The 'Strike of 400,000' is an exceptional moment in our understanding of the relationship between the workers and the so-called populist politicians. It exposes a working class in action, demanding their rights, requiring reciprocity from those who declared themselves to be in support of them.[19] It was not a breach opened by the division of the economic and political élite. The strike reaffirmed the workers' agency as well as their active and decisive role in that period.

The great weapon

The pickets had a determining role in the development of the 'Strike of 400,000'. They maintained a strong presence in the streets of the city and were fundamental to the success of the movement. Both participants and observers stressed their importance. Antonio Chamorro, veteran weavers' leader, in his speech on the last day of the stoppage, highlighted 'the work of the pickets, the great weapon of the strike'. The conservative newspaper *O Estado de São Paulo* admitted that 'the action of the pickets is more and more efficient. In 90 per cent of the cases the workers are persuaded by them to join in the strike'. The FIESP itself could not deny the evidence and revealed that most of 'our affiliates couldn't work due to the pickets'.[20]

Researchers of the working-class movement during the 1950s have also noted the importance of pickets in the strikes of that period. In a classic study about strikes in São Paulo, Leôncio Martins Rodrigues asserted that the pickets were 'the decisive tool in the success of the strikes'. According to him, the pickets were aimed mainly at the workers without organisation and traditions of collective action—the former, peasants newly integrated in the industrial world, who constituted the majority of the workers. The pickets, in his opinion, were the only possible organisers of a weak trade unionism with no representation in the workplace. The strikes were a 'movement provoked and achieved from the outside to the inside' of the firms.[21]

Nevertheless, a more detailed analysis of the strike and trade unionism at that time can reveal an alternative and more complex view of the pickets' role. They help us to understand better the workers' organisation and action during that period.

Many recent studies based on research about localities or about specific workers and trade unions have demonstrated that it is not possible to assume the complete absence of union organisation in the workplace between 1945 and 1964.[22] Despite the limitations imposed by the trade union structure, as well as the police and employers, many unions managed to develop some organisation inside companies.

The election of *delegados sindicais* (shop stewards) in the main industries of São Paulo became a common practice in the second half of the 1950s. A police spy in the metalworkers' union, for instance, concerned with the situation, claimed in his report that 'this trade union already has shop stewards in many companies'.[23]

Another example of organisation in the workplace was the 'dropper operation', unleashed by the São Paulo Textile Workers Union, after many companies had refused to pay the wage increase. This operation 'took the form of stoppages that lasted 15 minutes to one hour, and in some cases as often as four times per day'.[24] In one factory the managers tried unsuccessfully to identify the leaders of the movement, but the workers' answer was just: 'the leaders are the 25 per cent'. In this factory 'all workers that the boss judged to be shop stewards were suspended'.[25]

The shop stewards were the most regular union visitors and were always present at the meetings. They became a reference to the other workers and they, in many cases, were the link between what was happening inside the factories and the union leadership. They were chosen, in general, by 'secret and direct election among the workers of each industry'[26] and were a sort of channel of communication, taking the workers' demands and opinions to the union on a daily basis.

The very existence of these shop stewards, and their actions, challenge the arguments about the absence of a connection between the leadership and the rank and file of the unions, and the consequent lack of representation of the unionism of that period. Moreover, it could open other possible lines of analysis of the workers' actions and attitudes.

The shop stewards had a decisive role in the preparation and development of the 'Strike of 400,000'. They were usually the leaders of the pickets, and alongside their closest comrades in the factories constituted the nucleus of the pickets. Thus, during the strike, the first factories to be visited by pickets were those whose workers were more organised and closer to the unions, and the biggest ones. Next, they tried to bring to stoppage the smaller companies and those that were less organised by the unions.

In 1957, the success of the pickets was evident. The pickets occupied the streets of the industrial districts of São Paulo and these gatherings turned into huge workers' demonstrations. Rather than disperse, the workers on strike preferred to join in with the pickets. In the industrial neighbourhood of Bom Retiro, for instance, 'a picket with more than 10,000 strikers' was responsible for the stoppage of all metal, textiles and graphics industries located in that area. 'Like hundreds of lighted fuses at the same time, the strike spread quickly, reaching all neighbourhoods'.[27]

The so-called 'monster-pickets', gathering thousands of workers, were part of the leadership's strategy. 'We made three "monster-pickets"', a union activist remembers:

> We took our union flag. A splendid, big, red flag. We paraded in front of the factories and we made speeches for three hours. This picket was wonderful.[28]

Nevertheless, the presence of a group of migrant workers, newcomers from the rural areas, was concerning the leadership of the unions. Unskilled and without union experience, these workers, they believed, would be more susceptible to employers' pressure and also more afraid of unemployment. The communist newspaper, *Notícias de Hoje* (Daily News), for example, attempting to appeal to this group of workers, praised the strike and protests as the workers' weapons in the 'struggle for their rights':

> the grandparents of the grandparents, descendants of the Italians,

Spaniards, Germans and other immigrants, had also had this experience before. The peasants' sons and daughters who came to São Paulo have already understood it.[29]

In fact, the participation in the strike of young Northeastern migrants seemed to be as intense as that of the other workers' factions. Indeed, many factories that drew together great numbers of migrant workers, such as *Nitro Química*, were stopped.[30] The support of these workers pleased the leadership. A journalist on *Notícias de Hoje* euphorically reported the strike in a glass factory, *Wheathon do Brasil*, writing that the workers:

> were all Northeasterners and they already started to understand that the union, the struggle and the workers' organisation are necessary in order to obtain what made them leave their homes and villages where they were born.[31]

The ties of solidarity created from the common experience inside the factories and in workers' neighbourhoods, added to political and union militancy, were elements fundamental to the success of the movement. In this sense, the pickets were an essential tool. In addition, they had a strong demonstrative effect. A young worker explained what had led him to join the strike after the action of a picket, in these words:

> I thought that I should support the strike to follow my comrades. It is shameful to see your colleagues sacrificing themselves while you are doing nothing.[32]

Beyond the stimulation of class solidarity, the pickets also provided some protection against police and management repression. Within the pickets, the isolated worker felt stronger, the sense of community and identity enlarged.[33] Moreover, the pickets were an assurance to the workers that the strike was in fact taking place. They could join it without the risk of becoming alone. During the strike, the pickets were a quick and efficient form of communication among the workers in a city like São Paulo.[34] The enormous receptivity to the strike was beyond the forms of organisation created by the unions. A former leader of the pickets recalls that there were also 'natural pickets…they were the most efficient. They informed us whether the strike was increasing or decreasing'.[35] Initially, the pickets originated from the action of the union leadership, shop stewards and nucleus of workers linked with the unions, but during the strike, the voluntary participation of common workers reached impressive dimensions. Informal contact among workers was a really important way of increasing the movement.

> The majority participated for the first time in a picket. Their colleagues in the factories had introduced them....Many had tremendous success. I remember two of them. Wherever they went the workers were convinced to join the strike. And they didn't go to the factories by car....They went by bus and by tram.[36]

Fábio Munhoz, stressing the bureaucratic and controlling features of unionism at the time, argued about the appearance of what he called 'workers' spontaneousness' during the 'Strike of 400,000'. According to him this spontaneity threatened the union structure and ran against the unity of the union leaders who were aiming to preserve the 'trade union machine'.[37] Apart from the fact that this view does not take into account many formal and informal ties among the union leaders, militants and workers in general, this idea of 'spontaneity' underrates the organisational and mobilisation efforts built by the working class. Furthermore, this perspective highlights the view of a 'natural' workers' inclination to the struggle. It does not take into account the *historical* dimension of working-class organisation. In 1957, class mobilisation went beyond the unions' scope, but, even so, the unions were clearly considered by the workers as the main instrument of struggle and organisation of the strike.

The strike represented, on the one hand, an impulse issuing from the factories, workers' exploitation and the forms of organisation created or re-appropriated by the workers. On the other hand, the stoppages were also located in the workers' neighbourhoods and localities. In this sense, the pickets in 1957 must be seen as a sign of vitality, rather than weakness. In the 1950s, São Paulo was still a socially divided city. A famous statement made by the Mayor of New York, Fiorello LaGuardia, during the 1940s, was even more evident a decade later. Visiting São Paulo and viewing the city from the top of its highest building, LaGuardia, looking east, in the direction of the poorest neighbourhoods, said: 'In that part, people work.' Then, pointing to Paulista Avenue and nearby élite localities, he concluded: 'Over there, they eat.'[38] The accelerated growth of São Paulo during the 1950s resulted in a vast enlargement of the region where 'people work', and in new industrial zones, especially in the southern part of the city.

Lúcio Kowarick and Nabil Bonduki, Brazilian scholars specialising in São Paulo social movements and the urban history of the city, have pointed out how this period, and the occupation of the city outskirts by the workers, was characterised by the 'consolidation of a suburban pattern of urban sprawl' in São Paulo.[39] The low standard of living in those places and the almost complete absence of an urban infrastructure were part of the daily experience of thousands of people. However, in those neighbourhoods a range of popular organisations, such as tenant and neighbourhood organisations which demanded urban improvements, was being developed and was playing an important role in the political life of the city.

The trade unions and the strikes of this period cannot be separated from this general context. During the 'Strike of 400,000', for example, many neighbourhood associations supported the strikers. Moreover, the streets of 'working-class' neighbourhoods were the place where the strike and the workers' solidarity were forged. By comparing the strike of 1957 with another massive strike that took place in 1953, *Notícias de Hoje* pointed out that:

> the pickets, which in 1953 went out only from the trade unions, now arise from everywhere, on workers' own initiative. They bring the factories where they work to a stoppage spontaneously, and then they go united aiming at other industries. The pickets do not break up. This is another new feature of this strike.[40]

Leôncio Rodrigues considers the location of enterprises to be an important factor in the strike process. According to him, 'factories placed in workers' neighbourhoods...more easily led to stoppages'.[41] This point was not developed further by Rodrigues, but it appears to be an excellent clue to understanding the extent of popular participation in the 'Strike of 400,000'.

The English sociologist Michael Savage, among others, has pointed out the importance of space in the process of class formation. Space, as social network, can be the basis, the 'habitat', where collective action is created. However, space is not just the locus where class formation takes place, but it is itself part of the process. Thus, according to his view, working-class formation has a dual dynamic. It 'involves the construction of social networks of wide range, linking members of that class across different local sites', through trade unions and political parties, for instance, but also 'the construction of dense ties which allows the forging of solidaristic and communal identities over time and in absence of formal organisation. Here, classes can draw upon 'community', face-to-face relationships, which are conducive to social solidarity.'[42]

Savage's suggestions can be really useful to the analysis of the 'Strike of 400,000'. Face-to-face relationships and dense ties were present in the shop stewards' actions, with the union leaders in the factories, and in the common everyday experiences of thousands of workers. They rested on a 'local solidarity',[43] which was essential to the success of the movement. In one sense, the organisation and action of the pickets were related to this dynamic.

However, the strike and the pickets also had a wider dynamic. They united different professions and had the sympathy of the population in general. The PUI and the trade unions played a decisive role in the making of a movement, which went beyond local demands. They joined together through language against inflation and struggled for an equal and general wage rise for all, a wide-ranging solidarity and a class discourse that sent the workers into action.

Acknowledgements

The author would like to express his gratitude to Huw Beynon, Kevin Morgan and Neville Kirk for their comments on earlier versions of this article and for their encouragement. A version of this paper was published in Brazil ('Centenas de estopins acesos ao mesmo tempo. A greve dos 400 mil, piquetes e a organização dos trabalhadores em São Paulo', in A. Fortes et al., *Luta por Direitos. Estudos recentes em História Social do Trabalho* (Campinas, 1999). I also wish to thank Michael Hall, Alexandre Fortes, Antonio Negro, Fernando T. Silva, Hélio da Costa and Angela Silva.

Notes

1. Many politicians, among them the current president, have tried to associate their image with that of Kubitschek. In his first speech as president in 1995, Fernando Henrique Cardoso recalled 'Kubitschek's golden age' (*Folha de S. Paulo*, 2 November 1995). A month later, he visited the city where the former president was born and asserted: 'Kubitschek was a president who made history. If I do a bit of what he did, I will be happy.'(*Folha de S. Paulo*, 10 February 1995).
2. *O Observador Econômico e Financeiro*, October, 1957.
3. The best example of this perspective can be seen in Leôncio Martins Rodrigues, 'Greves operárias em São Paulo', in idem *Conflito Industrial e Sindicalismo no Brasil*, São Paulo, 1966. Another two specific articles about the 'Strike of 400,000' also stress the supposed bureaucratic features of the trade unionism of that period. See Fábio Munhoz, *Sindicalismo e Democracia Populista. A Greve de 1957* (São Paulo, 1977) and Márcia de Paula Leite, 'Trabalhadores, sindicatos e partidos: a greve de 1957 em São Paulo', in *El Sindicalismo Latino Americano em los Ochenta* (Santiago, 1985).
4. According to Paul Singer, between 1949 and 1959, average wages in the indus-

trial sector rose by 31 per cent, while average productivity rose by 138.5 per cent. See Paul Singer, *A Crise do 'Milagre'. Interpretação crítica da economia brasileira* (Rio de Janeiro, 1982), p.52.
5. The PUI was created after the 'Strike of 300,000' in 1953. The main unions of São Paulo belonged to it. According to union legislation in Brazil, union confederations were forbidden, but the law did not mention informal pacts between unions. Taking advantage of this omission, the trade union leaders created the PUI, which in practice worked as a confederation during the 1950s.
6. *Notícias de Hoje*, 13 October 1957.
7. University of the State of São Paulo (Unesp) Archives (hereafter CEDEM), Fábio Munhoz Collection, interview with a picket's leader, São Paulo Metalworkers' Union, 5 November 1958; and *Notícias de Hoje*, 10 October 1957.
8. National Archives of United States of America (Nara II), General Records of the Department of the State, RG 59, Central Decimal File, 1955–59, box 4310, 832.062/12–1057 (hereafter *The S. Paulo Strike of October 15–25, 1957*), p.5.
9. *Notícias de Hoje*, 9 October 1957.
10. Jânio Quadros is considered one of the best examples of a populist politician between the Second World War and the 1964 military coup in Brazil. He had a very impressive political career in the 1950s and 1960s. Councillor in São Paulo, he was elected Mayor of the city in 1954 using an anti-corruption discourse and an exotic style towards the workers and the poor. In 1956, he was elected Governor of the state and, eventually, in 1960, President of Brazil. However, in strange circumstances, which to the present day still have not been completely explained, he resigned seven months after his election, in 1961.
11. Fábio Munhoz, *Sindicalismo*, p.25.
12. Dissatisfied with the court decision, the employers appealed against the sentence in the Labour Federal Court. In January 1958, the Federal Court checked the regional decision and lowered the wage increase to 18 per cent. Apparently, however, most of the industries decided to maintain the former rise of 25 per cent in order to avoid new conflicts with the workers.
13. *The S. Paulo Strike of October 15–25, 1957*, p. 23.
14. Interview with Luis Tenório de Lima given to Paulo Fontes and Hélio da Costa, 8 September 1997. Police reports about the same meeting confirm de Lima's version. See Public Record Office of São Paulo (hereafter AESP), Social and Political Police records (hereafter DEOPS) sector, dossier 43–E–0 sheet 1,961.
15. *The S. Paulo Strike of October 15–25, 1957*, p.27 and *Notícias de Hoje*, 17 October 1957.
16. *Boletim Interno da FIESP/CIESP*, 8 January 1958.
17. *Notícias de Hoje*, 22 October 1957.
18. The women, as in other strikes in that period, were very active in 1957 and they had a fundamental role both in the factories and in the neighbourhoods. They participated actively in the pickets, especially in the textile factories, where women, in fact, were the majority of the labour force. In the working-class neighbourhoods they organised 'community meals' providing lunch and food-

stuffs to the strikers. I believe the unions' discourse against inflation and workers' poor standard of living had a special impact among the women. In most cases, they were responsible for shopping and controlling the domestic budget. For a general approach to women's role in the working-class movement during the 1940s and 1950s see Joel Wolfe, *Working Women, Working Men. São Paulo and the rise of Brazil's industrial working class, 1900–1955* (Durham, 1993) and Hélio da Costa, *Em Busca da Memória. Comissão de fábrica, partido e sindicato no pós-guerra* (São Paulo, 1995).

19. The expression 'populist political system' was coined by the historian John French, who emphasises the workers' action and criticises the notion of populism, as a relationship between charismatic politicians and subordinated workers can be useful for an understanding of the political landscape during the strike in 1957. See John French, *The Brazilian Workers' ABC. Class, conflict and alliances in modern São Paulo* (Chapel Hill, 1992).
20. See *Notícias de Hoje*, 25 October 1957; *O Estado de São Paulo*, 16 October 1957 and *Boletim Interno da FIESP/CIESP*, 28 October 1957.
21. Leôncio Martins Rodrigues, 'Greves', p.98 and pp.76–7.
22. See, among others, José Sérgio Leite Lopes, *A Tecelagem dos Conflitos de Classe na Cidade das Chaminés* (São Paulo, 1988); José Ricardo Ramalho, *Estado-patrão e Cultura Operária. O caso FNM* (Rio de Janeiro, 1989); Marco Aurélio, *Partido e Militância Sindical*, unpublished MA dissertation, Universidade do Rio de Janeiro, 1992; Wolfe, *Working*; da Costa, *Em Busca*; French, *The Brazilian*; Fernando Teixeira da Silva, *A Carga e a Culpa. Os operários das docas de Santos: direitos e cultura de solidariedade* (São Paulo, 1995); Paulo Fontes, *Trabalhadores e Cidadãos. Nitro Química: a fábrica e as lutas operárias nos anos 50* (São Paulo, 1997) and Marcelo Badaró Mattos, *Novos e Velhos Sindicalismos no Rio de Janeiro (1955–1988)* (Rio de Janeiro, 1998).
23. AESP, DEOPS sector, dossier 50–Z–318, sheet 2,886.
24. *The S. Paulo Strike of October 15–25, 1957*, p.31 and AESP, DEOPS sector, dossier 50–A–1, sheet 110.
25. *Notícias de Hoje*, 11 December 1957.
26. CEDEM, Fábio Munhoz Collection, interview with a picket leader, São Paulo Metalworkers' Union, 5 November 1958.
27. *Notícias de Hoje*, 17 October 1957 and 16 October 1957.
28. CEDEM, Fábio Munhoz Collection, interview with a picket leader, São Paulo Glass Workers' Union, October 1958.
29. *Notícias de Hoje*, 15 October 1957.
30. For a specific analysis of the *Nitro Química* strike, see Fontes, *Trabalhadores*, pp.143–79.
31. *Notícias de Hoje*, 26 October 1957.
32. *Notícias de Hoje*, 16 October 1957.
33. Huw Beynon, analysing an assembly of metalworkers in the automobile industry, points out the importance of massive demonstrations to the unskilled workers. See Huw Beynon, *Working for Ford* (1973). Michelle Perrot also

observes how the strikes and its manifestations are important in reducing the workers' isolation in the labour process, to dilute their internal differences and to emphasise their condition as workers. See Michelle Perrot, *Workers on Strike. France 1871–1890* (New York, 1987).
34. According to the Statistical Department of São Paulo State, the city of São Paulo had 3,318,569 inhabitants in 1957. In 1956, according to the newspaper *A Gazeta* (17 April 1957), there were 22,788 industries, with an average of 22 workers in each workplace.
35. CEDEM, Fábio Munhoz Collection, interview with a picket leader, São Paulo Glass Workers' Union, October 1958.
36. Ibid.
37. Fábio Munhoz, *Sindicalismo*, p.27.
38. Quoted in Joel Wolfe, ' "Father of the poor" or "Mother of the Rich"?: Getúlio Vargas, industrial workers, and populism in São Paulo, 1930–1954', *Radical History Review*, vol. 58 (1994).
39. Lúcio Kowarick and Nabil Bonduki, 'Espaço urbano e espaço político: do populismo à redemocratização', in Lúcio Kowarick (ed.), *As Lutas Sociais e a Cidade—São Paulo. Passado e presente* (Rio de Janeiro, 1988), p.142.
40. *Notícias de Hoje,* 18 October 1957.
41. Rodrigues, 'Greves', p.80.
42. Michael Savage, 'Space, networks and class formation', in Neville Kirk (ed.), *Social Class and Marxism. Defences and challenges* (Hants, 1996).
43. Analysing many studies about the relationship between community and working class in the US, UK, France and Germany, David Crew points out that class solidarity can not be understood just as a 'natural product of the community'. Class solidarity 'when and where it existed, was not the product of ecological factors but of deliberate human efforts.' See David Crew, 'Class and community. Local research on working-class history in four countries', *Historische Zeitschrift*, vol. 15 (1986), p.300.

Design for Utopia?

David Grove

'People make cities but cities make citizens'. Those are the first words—and also the last—of the recent interim report by Richard Rogers' Urban Task Force.[1] They suggest a dialectical relationship between people and places that ought to be central to the concept of utopia.

I began trying to explore that relationship in the late 1930s when I was becoming aware of a world beyond the rather dreary Liverpool suburb where I grew up. Our cleaning lady had been moved to a council house under a slum clearance scheme. She used to tell us that her neighbours didn't like their new homes and hankered after the old slums.

This puzzled me—until I came across a book in the school library called *Poverty and Public Health* by McGonigle and Kirby. It was a study of a slum clearance scheme at Stockton-on-Tees. The startling finding was that when families were moved from crumbling terraces in the inner area, with primitive sanitary arrangements and tiny back yards, to semi-detached houses with gardens on the edge of town...the death rate and the disease rate both went *up*. The researchers identified the main reasons for this as: higher rents, extra heating costs, extra costs of travel to work or to sign on for the dole, and higher prices in suburban shops. All this additional expenditure led to a fall in the quantity and quality of their food, and so to more sickness and earlier death. I can't remember whether the authors also mentioned additional stress resulting from the break-up of the old slum community, but I would now suggest that as another important factor.

Reading *Poverty and Public Health* set me feeling a way towards a materialist analysis of the interaction between social relations and the built environment. As you'll find out, I'm still feeling my way.

Now nobody would claim that slum clearance was much of a step towards utopia. But like utopia, it entailed a form of social engineering; it sought to change people's life style by changing their surroundings.

About the same time that I read *Poverty and Public Health* I read a book on town planning by a Labour MP whose name I forget—it was a Scottish name. He extolled the virtues of Welwyn Garden City—the utopia of the day—and among other things pointed out that the death rates were significantly lower than in inner London. But by now I was smart enough to know that this wasn't mainly because of the clean air and civic amenities but because more people in Welwyn had jobs and decent incomes, many indeed commuting to London.

Now of course Ebenezer Howard, founder of Letchworth and Welwyn, knew very well that the social changes he envisaged depended on more than the location and layout of a town. He was a genuine utopian in the sense that he pictured a transformed society. In his diagram of the three magnets, he thought the people would be attracted to Garden City rather than to existing urban or rural areas not just by 'bright homes and gardens, pure air and water', but as well by 'low rents and high wages, no sweating, social opportunity' and so on. He even wrote that Garden City would show 'how the bounds of freedom may be widened, and yet all the best results of concert and cooperation gathered in by a happy people.'[2]

But it was not to be a total transformation; Howard expected capitalist social relations to remain. Indeed, he saw his book, originally subtitled *A Peaceful Path to Real Reform*, as an answer to socialist utopias, especially that of Edward Bellamy, but also that of William Morris. So the famous magnet promises 'flow of capital and field for enterprise'.

Howard believed that capitalism would build garden cities. But he knew this could happen only if land were acquired at knock down prices as a result of the agricultural depression, and if enough wealthy men settled for five per cent philanthropy—both unlikely in the long run. And not even Howard's eloquence could show how a capitalist economy could guarantee full employment and high wages.

The slow growth of Letchworth and Welwyn, the failure to build more garden cities, and the deficiencies of slum clearance were among the reasons for Labour's victory in 1945. Housing was one of the four big issues that put Labour into power, and when during the war people expressed their aspirations for housing they almost always included better town planning and urban design as essential elements in the post-war world. So we got the 1946 New Towns Act and utopia was on the agenda again.

When I went to work in Crawley in 1951, the old village was encircled by building sites, houses were just coming on stream, and a big engineering works was about to move from London. Every weekend a fleet of coaches brought factory workers to tour the town and study the plans. They were offered a choice of perhaps three or four house types in two or three neighbourhoods—but they were never asked for their own views on the design of homes or the layout of residential areas.

At the Development Corporation there were earnest young social science graduates carefully studying the literature on what people needed by way of open spaces, meeting places, and so on—but they never went out and asked the people what they would like.

Social engineering again—and from the top down—as in most utopias, with the conspicuous exceptions of Morris's and I suppose Winstanley's. Most fictional utopias have been put in place by a Prince and/or Philosophers. The new towns had both.

In Crawley the Prince was a two-headed monster: the Chairman and the Chief Executive. The chairman was an architect who ran a large practice with commissions mainly from big business; the chief executive was a colonel, a chartered accountant and chartered surveyor who later became a partner in one of the leading commercial estate agents. Similar people ran all the new towns. They were accountable only to Whitehall. Local authorities had no say but were expected to provide all the usual services.

Like Howard, the Princes saw the need for a flow of capital—but there was to be no philanthropy. Whether private or public, all investment was to yield a commercial return. The Crawley chairman said that industrialists 'moving into the area have universally informed us that their production is higher, their sickness and accident rates are lower, and the interest of workers in production shows a very marked improvement'.[3] So good housing, contented families and a short bike ride to work resulted in a marked increase in the rate of exploitation of the labour force!

Howard would not have been surprised. But he would have regretted that wages were not higher nor rents and rates lower. Indeed, both rents and rates were above those elsewhere. For many years new town residents paid higher than average local taxes per head for a lower level of services.

The Philosophers saw things differently; they were the idealistic young architects, planners, sociologists and other experts, most of whom were keen to assist at the birth of a new way of life. But the initiative still came from the top. They were experts in the paternalistic Fabian tradition, which—let's face it—most of us professionals were imbued with at the time. They hoped that in the congenial setting of the new neighbourhoods everybody would turn to creative activity and social responsibility. In fact, almost the opposite happened. With the advent of TV and with skilled workers able to afford washing machines and cars, life in the new towns became more home- and family-centred. New town managers and the Treasury discouraged risky innovations. So there were few architectural or social experiments, nothing so forward-looking as, for instance, the Peckham Health Centre and the Cambridgeshire community colleges, both from the 1930s.

Ironically, the very conditions that gave rise to higher productivity in the factories also generated greater militancy among the workers. The solidarity of the workplace was carried into the neighbourhoods. There were epic struggles against rent increases and redundancies, and for the timely building of the schools, hospitals and other facilities shown on the excellent master plans. So after all the people did play a part in shaping the new towns.

Socially and economically the new towns have become much like any others. If you're unemployed or struggling to live on a low wage, if you're overworked and insecure, I don't suppose you feel a lot nearer to utopia in a new town than anywhere else. All the same, as I wrote in *Marxism Today* in 1962, the new towns offer 'a better environment than capitalism has ever before provided for a large number of working people';[4] I think that judgment still stands up. With their neighbourhood centres, generous open space, safe walkways and cycleways, the new towns are—it seems to me—the best vindication of positive and comprehensive planning.

But are they good enough for Morris's 'epoch of rest'? Perhaps they should be seen as an instalment—or a component—of utopia. Can there be instalments of utopia? It seems like an all-or-nothing concept. The classic utopias were a way of describing a better society at a time when the social forces to realise it didn't exist.

But if—as Morris hoped—the dream can now become a vision, then perhaps partial realisations may be helpful. Leslie Morton wrote: 'It seems likely that much of the thought and energy that once went into the fabrication of paper utopias will go into more practical and more satisfying tasks.' But he added: 'the problems of the future are perennially fascinating…and I think we may well see socialist utopias which trace lines of possible development'.[5] Morton was probably thinking of literary works, but his remark may be even more relevant to experiments in moulding the physical environment, which besides offering guidance and inspiration can perhaps give a foretaste of the future too.

So—to return to my starting point—what can we expect—or what should we demand—of the Urban Renaissance that Prescott has asked Rogers to mastermind? The Task Force—which will report any day now—has ambitious terms of reference: to 'establish a new vision for urban regeneration founded on the principles of design excellence, social well-being and environmental responsibility within a viable economic and legislative framework'. That goes far beyond just the shaping of the built environment. Yet Rogers wrote in the interim report that their 'remit is primarily a physical one, about buildings and spaces'. Perhaps he thus limited the scope of the task force because he believes in architectural determinism, or perhaps because he can't imagine much progress in tackling the underlying problems of poverty and insecurity so long as capitalist social reforms prevail.

Still, there is a real possibility of marked changes in the form of urban development in order to provide the 4 million or so additional homes said to be needed in the next 20 years, while trying to reconcile the many conflicting interests that will be affected. The discussion is well under way, in professional circles and far beyond them, on greenfield or brownfield land, new settlements or expansion of existing ones, density and parking standards, and other relevant considerations. Can our past attempts at shaping utopia make a contribution that might result in a few more instalments of the future urban scene?

It seems to be that any serious strategy is bound to include some new towns, perhaps to absorb most of the building on greenfield land. As things stand, private capital is likely to have a leading role. Can this be combined with the full involvement of local councils and with genuine public participation? The Task Force is into the consultation business—but its approach seems to be the fashionable one of using commercial marketing techniques like focus groups, designed to find out what can be sold to potential customers rather than democratic discussion designed to reach a consensus among free citizens.

Can another generation of new towns, building on the achievements of the earlier ones, pioneer new urban forms where people will enjoy enough private space while feeling part of a local community, will they own cars yet make most of their journeys to work, schools, shops and services on foot or cycle, bus or train? If they can, then they may indeed bring us some instalments of utopia that can help to show people how different life might be in a socialist city.

But as well as building new towns we must at the same time put equivalent resources into remodelling much of our existing urban fabric with similar objectives. Otherwise, another generation of new towns will contribute to the decay of the inner cities, just as the earlier new towns did.

But I can't help observing that the opportunities both for building new towns and rebuilding old ones are fewer than they've been for many years, while the constraints—political, social and economic—are much greater. One of the main constraints is of course the private ownership of most of the land on which building must take place. It is hard to conceive of a utopia in which the land is not owned by the communities that occupy it. It is possible that land could be taken into common ownership even within a capitalist framework. I believe the 1945 Labour government could have done it if they'd had the clarity and courage. Will it be politically possible in the near future? It may well be that this is one of the most important battles to be won in the campaign to create some more instalments of the built environment of utopia.

This article is based on a talk given at a joint meeting of the Socialist History Society and Democratic Left Architecture and Planning Group, Letchworth, 12 June 1999.

Notes

1. *Urban Renaissance. Sharing the vision*, DETR, January 1999, pp.3, 55.
2. Ebenezer Howard, *Tomorrow! A Peaceful Path to Real Reform* (London, 1898).
3. Sir Thomas Bennett, *Address*, 9 April 1960 (Crawley, 1960), p.10.
4. David Grove, 'Lessons of the new towns', *Marxism Today*, vol. 6, no. 3 (1962), p.87.
5. Leslie Morton, 'Utopia yesterday and today' in Margot Heinemann and Willie Thompson (eds), *History and the Imagination* (London, 1990).

Reviews

South African communism

Dale T. McKinley, *The ANC and the Liberation Struggle: A critical political biography* (Pluto Press, London, 1997), xv & 160 pp., ISBN 0-7453-1282-9 hbk, 0-7453-1277-2 pbk.

This book, written by a member of the South African Communist Party (SACP), seeks to explain why the South African liberation struggle failed to produce any genuine socio-economic transformation for the majority of the people. Through an examination of the African National Congress (ANC) and its relationship with the SACP, Dale McKinley argues that the ANC's strategy consistently undermined the possibility for social transformation by downgrading the significance of its working-class base. The ANC's strategy was based on a two-stage theory of revolution which 'allowed for a conceptual division between apartheid and capitalism', McKinley writes. 'The result of this tactic was to lead to a strategic alliance with important sections of capital against the apartheid state' (p.75). Hence, the ANC's failure to promote transformation.

McKinley's main focus is the last three decades of exile and armed struggle and, finally, of negotiations for the democratic transition. However, he traces the roots of the ANC's strategic orientation back to the 1920s and 1930s. Problems in his handling of history are apparent at the outset. He writes that '[b]ecause of the incredibly close relationship between the SACP and the ANC since 1950 (when the SACP [sic] was banned), it should be noted that I will not always distinguish between the two, but rather use the term ANC to encompass the SACP as well'. He uses both names only when, in his view, it is necessary to demarcate the divergent policies and activities of both organizations (p.x). He asserts that although socialism has been 'associated more with the SACP and COSATU (Congress of South African

Trade Unions) than with the ANC itself, there has been such an overlap of membership that to disassociate the goal of socialism from the ANC is a misdirected and convenient omission' (p.xi). This is not because the ANC itself has been socialist, he adds, but because many of its members have had a socialist outlook.

But such propositions need to be demonstrated. To project the present relationship between the SACP and the ANC back into the past leads to a tautological history. The SACP's predecessor, the Communist Party of South Africa (CPSA) did not subsume its own strategy to that of the ANC. Nor do the ideological stances of some of an organisation's members necessarily imply anything about the organisation's broader position or its political potential. Many—arguably most—of the ANC's members supported capitalism, after all. Indeed, McKinley himself characterises the ANC as petty bourgeois (p.13).

Chapter 1, 'The Formative Years', presents a simplistic overview of black working-class development. It assumes a linear proletarianisation and, in turn, a straightforward development of black working-class consciousness and organisation. This neglects the partial proletarianisation of the majority of South Africans—a result of earlier governments' restrictions on the movement of Africans to towns through the pass and migrant labour systems. Black political consciousness, both urban and rural, was far from uniform and was contested. The rather offhand statement that '[t]here was also some organisation among the white working class' (p.8) gives a misleading impression. For historical reasons, white working-class organisation preceded black working-class organisation—with important political consequences.

McKinley's characterisation of the early CPSA is problematic. The assertion that 'some of the early "communists" were no less racist than those they wanted to replace' (p.8) is contentious. There is no doubt that many early white Communists were paternalistic in their attitudes towards blacks. But they were far less racist than most other white South Africans, including those in the whites-only South African Labour Party. The claim that white Communists marched under a banner calling for a white South Africa (p.8) is at best dubious. The notorious slogan of the 1922 Rand Revolt, 'Workers of the World Fight and Unite for a White SA' (misquoted in the text), appeared on a banner held up, the historical record suggests, by white mineworkers and their wives. There appears to be no evidence, to date, that the CPSA supported this slogan—indeed, to the contrary—or that communists marched under the banner.

The mid-1930s saw the formation of new black political alliances, including the formation of the All African Convention (AAC). McKinley's interpretation of this development, together with his claim that '[o]ne of the more significant results of this opening up was to put the ANC, for the first time, in at least indirect alliance with the Communist Party' (p.10), is dubious. The AAC represented a broad democratic alliance—it is teleological to find within that alliance the seeds of the ANC's subsequent alliance with the Communist Party. It is inaccurate to describe the CPSA as the ANC's 'alliance partner' (p.11) during the years 1936–45. The characterisation of the CPSA as 'dutifully' following Moscow's dictates in adopting the 'people's front' policy in the late 1930s is simplistic. The discussion of the CPSA's 'people's front' is misleading—its adoption did not mean that the CPSA construed socialism as 'a mostly foreign (white) ideology which was not appropriate to "African conditions"' as McKinley suggests (p.11). His conclusion that, by the late 1940s, the outcome of the ANC's and CPSA's politics was 'the decisive defeat of a working-class-led [sic] socialist alternative to African nationalism in the struggle for South African liberation' (p.13) is question begging. First, was there such a socialist alternative to be defeated in the 1940s? CPSA membership had plummeted to less than 100 in the 1930s and, despite a substantial increase in numbers due to an accommodation with the government's war efforts, CPSA membership was fewer than 2000 at its dissolution in 1950. Second, McKinley's explanation for this defeat—that the CPSA 'chose to integrate itself so closely with the ANC and thus to identify with the decidedly petit-bourgeois character of that movement' (p.13)—is false. In the 1940s the CPSA pursued a distinctive agenda and did not have a tightly integrated relationship with the ANC.

The book contains numerous specific errors. For instance, the Congress Alliance of the 1950s did not include the Federation of South African Women (p.19); the SACP was formed in 1953, not 1959 (p.32); *Inkatha* is misspelled throughout; the Growth, Employment and Redistribution strategy adopted by the South African government in 1996 is mistitled (p.141, n.6).

On this inadequately researched and questionable understanding of the past, McKinley bases his assessment of the more recent relationship between the ANC and the SACP. He points to a series of lost opportunities in which the ANC failed to nurture and promote working-class activity. During the phase of armed struggle, for instance, *Umkhonto we Sizwe* (MK)—the ANC's armed struggle wing—relied on hit-and-run sabotage rather than developing a guerrilla strategy aimed at a seizure of power. '[A]s long as an externalised ANC leadership and strategy and tactics guided MK practice', he maintains, 'the scope for developing the conditions for an armed seizure of power was extremely limited' (p.79).

As a result of the obvious limitations in this approach to armed struggle, McKinley argues, ANC leaders opted, in the changing international climate of the late 1980s, for a negotiated settlement. But they presented this choice as a seemingly inevitable '"new terrain of struggle" for power, whose character and direction would be "determined by the masses"', rather than as their own strategic decision (p.100). In the early 1990s ANC leaders repeatedly dampened the militant spirit of the mass movement, confirming, in McKinley's view, 'the primacy of a bounded strategic approach to mass struggle and a dominant politics of accommodation' (p.126). For McKinley, current political outcomes are a legacy of the two-stage theory of revolution. 'Looking at the broader historical framework of the ANC's liberation struggle in which this perspective was regularly applied', he concludes, 'it becomes clear why a gradual disempowerment of the masses emerged and ultimately an increasingly truncated liberation' (p.129).

While not underestimating the need to critically interrogate the ANC's post-apartheid policies and to examine the history and trajectory of the liberation movement, this is a deeply flawed book. McKinley applies a schematic model to the past, squeezing history to fit the parameters of the model, in order to explain the ANC's failure to promote socio-economic transformation. However important strategy is, human activity does not flow from a script. McKinley does not consider difficult questions concerning the range of possibilities at particular moments or the choices that individuals, parties or movements made within those constraints. Any critical evaluation of contemporary South Africa must surely be based on an accurate and historically grounded understanding of the past.

Allison Drew
Department of Politics, University of York

Futures and pasts

Tim Jordan and Adam Lent (eds) *Storming the Millennium: The new politics of change* (Lawrence & Wishart, London, 1999), 218 pp., ISBN 0-85315-873-8.

What does it mean to be radical today, when we have witnessed/suffered this decade along the radical right and more recently the radical centre? 'The idea of difference is essential to any form of new politics', writes one of the editors, Tim Jordan (p.6). This collection from academics and activists (and activist-academics) presents a wider range of case studies than simply looking at lifestyle politics.

Links are traced between identity politics and the body in, for instance, chapters on disability movements and on dance culture. The connection could be pursued further: one preferred form of political activism today, direct action, is specifically about placing the body in an obstructive, delaying, visible (up a tree) or invisible (down a tunnel) position. Peter Beresford explains how disability movements have sought to challenge majority culture's views on disabled people: 'the social model of disability...draws a distinction between a disabled person's individual impairment...and "disability", which means: "all the things which impose restrictions on disabled people"' (p.36). Other essays interrogate the legacy of essentialism. Merl Storr explores the legacy of feminist and gay rights movements from the 1960s. She contends that the (perhaps) new identity of 'queer' rejects challenges the 1960s/1970s binaries of gay/straight, gay/lesbian: 'It is no longer simply a matter of dealing with multiple axes of oppression or with the complexities of being simultaneously oppressed along one axis (black, disabled)' (p.53). In another essay problematising the 1960s New Left's relatively uncomplicated monoliths of oppression and emancipation, Shirin Housee and Sanjay Sharma explore the current diversity of the signifier 'Black', in part by comparing it with 'Asian', an identity implicated in imperial/colonial history. The aim is to reclaim the category Asian, while ensuring that 'the unique moment of "Black" in the making of anti-racist political identities in Britain should not be so readily erased from memory in a rush to embrace and celebrate more contemporaneous and heterogeneous formations of identity' (p.121).

In a fascinating and wide-ranging interview with the editors of the culture and politics journal *Soundings*, Stuart Hall, Doreen Massey and Michael Rustin, the frequent claim of newness, one repeated in this book's subtitle, is interrogated. Talking about the Labour Party and the trade unions, Hall reminds us that sometimes 'we forget that what are now called the old social movements had a new social movement phase...we have to be careful about counterposing it as a simple old/new, then/now, gone/emerging set of oppositions' (pp.196–7). Michael Rustin identifies 'the worn qualities of the old discourse' of the left: 'Clearly there is a point at which a discourse becomes so tarnished or lifeless that one is better off not using it at all, and starting again' (p.204).

Indeed, the book contains examples of such discursive starting again, a change in terminology. Adam Lent's welcome critical chapter on strategic weaknesses and organisational divisions within new and historical movements alike revisits the old left divide between revolutionary and reformist by calling them the transformatory and the temperate. One conclusion he offers is hardly earth-shattering: 'some people are simply more inclined to fight and some to compromise' (p.174). The strength of the discussion lies in the fact that Lent traces the problem back—that is, tells a critical rather than celebratory history—and clearly weaves it together with a focus on what he takes to be the subjective turn in activism. For Lent then, for instance, DIY Culture of the 1990s (such as road protest or rave culture's anti-Criminal Justice Act activism of 1993–94) is an example of the third way (sorry): not transformatory, not temperate, but what he calls the personal-local. This is a different, altogether more individual response to unsatisfactory conditions: 'the change involves enhancement of self-confidence, self-reliance and self-respect, improved understanding of one's own motivations, goals and place in the world' (p.176). Locating such fluffy-sounding rhetoric in the context of collective action and the challenge to everyday life prevents it from being too much of a paean to the me-generation or indeed the e-generation. Lent explains that all three forms of world-view contribute energy and viability to political movements.

I would have liked here, as elsewhere throughout the book in fact, to see greater engagement with the long-standing political tradition that has for centuries preferred direct action (not always non-violent), has sought decentred and non-hierarchical forms of organisation, has interrogated and/or romanticised the revolutionary subject, the individual, has had as its great strength and weakness alike a focus on the local, the micro-political. I'm talking of course about anarchism, which is mentioned by several contributors (though not enough to warrant an index entry), occasionally in passing towards a longer, less interesting section on something to do with the failures of Marxism.

In spite of itself almost, on occasion the book betrays quite a traditional left construction of present-day political activism. For instance, Jordan's chapter on the old universal of class notes that 'Left, or liberatory politics is confused about which activities are liberatory and which are not' (pp.144–5). He offers the contemporary example of the animal liberation movement as a site of the left's confusion about the validity current activism, 'one area of undoubtedly active politics' (p.145). There is, however, no chapter on or extended discussion of animal liberation in the book—hardly the way to clear up the left's confusion about the subject. Or is it that animal rights are simply not considered sufficiently universal, even within the revised framework of universals that Jordan explores? Since the book raises the issue as a significant lacuna, I would expect it not to replicate that critical absence.

The critical issues and absences I have discussed should not obscure the book's currency and significance. *Storming the Millennium* captures the energy and much of the breadth of political activism in Britain today, interrogates the strengths and limitations of single issue and identity politics, and presents both theoretical and historical ways of understanding, of moving on. It is essential reading. After all, as Tim Jordan says in his introduction, in that combination of truism and melodrama characteristic of the rhetoric of alternative politics: '"Now" is always a good time to stand up and fight for your life' (p.1).

George McKay
Reader in Contemporary Cultural Studies at the University of Central Lancashire

Organising the internet

Eric Lee *The Labour Movement and the Internet* (Pluto Press, London, 1997), 256pp., ISBN 0-7453-1114-8, £14.99 pbk.

The working classes have always had an uneasy relationship with technology, and not without reason. During the Industrial Revolution, Luddites failed to prevent new technologies taking their jobs, and during the 1980s, print workers reacted in a similar fashion, as new printing technologies, and the use of palpably devious tactics by Rupert Murdoch, resulted in mass redundancies. Many aspects of Britain's restructuring can be seen as affected by technological change, if only indirectly. From the motor industry through to mining and textiles, technology has had a negative effect for the working class and trade unions.

Given this unfortunate relationship, it is a reasonable concern that the latest development in information and communications technology, the internet, will be viewed with similar fear and loathing. Fortunately, this doesn't seem to be the case. The TUC, for instance, have been commendable in their approach to the internet having created a vast interactive web site and recently an e-mail system to register votes on TUC business. Eric Lee is a pioneer of using the internet as a tool to benefit organised labour. Having been computer programmer, trade-union activist, and editor of trade-union journals, Lee is in an ideal position to write on the subject of the *Labour Movement and the Internet*, and he uses this experience to great effect.

Lee has provided a useful historical narrative of the development of the internet as a tool of trade unions. Although his subjective position negates any attempt at academic rigor, it is, nonetheless, a useful introduction to a subject area that will no doubt become more important to historians as we move further and further into the 'information age'.

The book begins with the assertion that labour and socialist Internationals have been in decline for the past century and that this is reflected in a reduced ability of trade unions to organise across boarders at a time when global capitalism is becoming increasingly integrated, organised and powerful. He argues that the internet, whose nature is global, non-hierarchical and borderless, can help reinvigorate internationalism, and ease the co-ordination of action and resistance by trade unions on the global level at which the corporations play.

The blurb on the back of the book claims that it is 'the first guide to the new electronic medium written specifically for trade unionists worldwide', and in keeping with this claim, Lee moves on to introduce the main components of the internet, and the tools with which workers and unions can communicate. The following section, and the bulk of the book, is set aside to developing an historical narrative of ways in which the tools assessed earlier have been employed in various circumstances from the development of the first national labournets to web-based strike papers. Lee paints a picture of employers' resistance to new technological innovation countered by the persistence of union technophiles and the general success of such efforts. The variety of examples illustrate under which circumstances particular internet tools have utility, and in which circumstances they have been less useful. Lee's approach is enthusiastic, but not naïve.

Interestingly and importantly, Lee wrestles with many of the problems that his claims, or desires, raise. The internet and local networks are available to only a tiny minority of people around the globe, and most of the people who can access it reside in the wealthiest nations, which usually have significant physical trade-union networks in place. Lee's remedy to this fact is that global capital is shifting away from Western Europe and North America, and that this shift will bring with it a corresponding shift in the centre of gravity for the trade-union movement, and in access to the internet. Such an assertion is, however, very controversial. It is simply not the case that areas outside the triad of the European Union, North America and Japan are receiving significant amounts of inward investment, or technological development. The expansion of the internet into the third world is not a foregone conclusion. Nevertheless, it is not the case that Lee fails to admit this, but rather that his method of dealing with the problems is unsophisticated and presumptuous. What is true though, is that computer-mediated global trade-union activity is feasible if the unions will it. As Lee questions: 'Is there a place for the labour movement in the new world order?

There is if labour chooses to make a place for itself?'

Lee has embarked upon what is initially a promising project, but he seems to have not exploited his ideas to the full. Although mainly a narrative work, his analysis of the subject is illustrative and factual but perhaps a little too superficial and, given that it is mainly descriptive, it would have been useful for him to include a more substantial prescriptive counterpart. For example, his approach to the effect of the internet on trade-union organisation is decidedly conservative, arguing that although computer networks have had a democratising effect, they have reinforced the existing trade-union structures. An analysis of how trade unions may be changed by the use of the internet would have been more ambitious and insightful. This conservative approach negated the possibility of a critique of current union organisation.

To be sure, the book is an interesting discussion. Technology is often overlooked, or viewed negatively, by sectors of the left so it is refreshing to see someone promoting its implementation as a tool of class struggle, as ownership of the means of production used to be. Lee does show some foresight in proposing three projects to revive internationalism. The first and second are interlinked and involve a global publishing and conferencing network, and the third proposes a global trade-union rights early-warning system so activists can mobilise around the world when companies or governments threaten workers' organisation. He presents these ideas in the final section on the re-emergence of the International but, unfortunately, ties the impact of the internet to previous forms of union activity and organisation. Rather than advocate social shaping of the internet to provide a radical horizontal arrangement of workers, Lee argues that the use of the internet by trade unions should remain along a vertical axis. A regurgitation of previous forms of activism and organisation and their arrangement in electronic form is perhaps too short sighted to make a positive contribution to the future of trade unionism.

Lee Salter, University of North London

International communisms

Tauno Saarela and Kimmo Rentola (eds), *Communism National and International*, Studia Historica 58; Helsinki, Suomen Historiallinen Seura 1998. ISSN 0081-6493; ISBN 951-710-079-5

Labour and socialist history is taken seriously in Finland. The archives and records of radical movements are held in conditions which can only arouse the envy of researchers from Britain. *Communism National and International*, published in English by the Finnish Historical Society, reflects this serious approach. Considerable effort has clearly been exerted to make this collection of conference papers accessible to as wide a readership as possible.

The conference in Helsinki at which these papers were first presented sought to explore the relationship between international (primarily Soviet) and national factors in communist history. Naturally enough, the book's main focus is on Finnish communism, although individual papers deal with France, Italy, Britain, and Scandinavia, as well as with aspects of Soviet ideology and policy.

In many respects, the tensions and conflicts between domestic and international pressures affected the Communist Party of Finland (SKP) in much the same way as they affected other European communist movements. Finnish communists were obliged to reconcile their own assessments of their domestic political situation with the policies and directives emanating from Moscow, with all the problems this occasionally entailed. In other respects, however, the Finnish situation was uniquely difficult.

First, many Finns saw communism as a real threat to Finland's very existence as an independent state. The Finns had wrested their independence from Petrograd in 1917. Although Finland's secession had been recognised by Lenin's government in January 1918, it was the military defeat of the Finnish Reds later that year which ensured that the country was not brought back into Russia's orbit. The SKP, founded in Moscow in August 1918, was more vulnerable than many parties to the charge that it was an agency of Russian policy. Second, the USSR had a significant Finnish population in the border region of Karelia, and, as the paper by Markku Kangaspuro shows, Finnish communist politics became intertwined with Soviet internal politics in this area, ultimately to the detriment of the Finns.

Finland's most notable contribution to world communism was the figure of Otto Kuusinen, a leader of the Finnish social democrats from 1905, and of the Reds in 1918. In exile in the USSR, he rose to important positions in the Comintern and later in the CPSU. In 1939, he headed the fictitious puppet government set up in Moscow to sanction the Soviet attack on Finland. This ensured that, unlike such figures as Togliatti and Dimitrov, Kuusinen could not return to his native country after the war and lead his now legal and powerful party. He was an inveterate survivor who, unlike many of his family, was not incarcerated during the Stalinist terror of the late 1930s. Incidentally, Kimmo Rentola's essay on Kuusinen contains a striking insight into that terror, which claimed an estimated 20,000 Finnish communists. Rentola likens it to a 'family matter' which left 'in the collective mentality of

Finnish communism an imprint comparable to the effects of child abuse on individual development. It was a close and dirty secret, necessary to keep out of view and of mind.'

An altogether more positive note is struck by the pieces dealing with the SKP inside Finland. Ulla-Maija Peltonen's survey of communist reminiscences from the 1920s and 1930s, and Elina Katainen's study of communist women's periodicals show how traditions of struggle and a vision of a better life were sustained in a very hostile environment.

The pieces in this book concerning parties other than the SKP adopt a variety of different angles. Kevin Morgan's study of Harry Pollitt and the CPGB examines the influence of the indigenous culture of the British labour movement upon the party. He warns against concentrating too exclusively on the influence of the Comintern in shaping the development of the CPGB. Aldo Agosti's paper on Palmiro Togliatti traces the relationship between his position as a trusted Comintern functionary and the post-war development of a more 'democratic' orientation within the Italian CP. The idea of the 'nation' is the central focus of Marc Lazar's piece on the French CP (PCF), in an exploration of that party's simultaneous devotion to the USSR and its sometimes immoderate nationalist or 'nationalitarian' (his word) impulses. The key factor is France's unusually rich revolutionary history, to which the PCF could see itself as the legitimate heir.

Morten Thing's study of 'Language and Communism', based mainly on the example of the Danish CP (DKP), explores how the ostensibly international language of communism acquired different connotations in different cultures. For example, in 1936 the DKP publisher got into trouble with the Comintern for omitting some of the more grotesque and, to a Danish readership, off-putting examples of 'thunderous ovation' from one of Stalin's speeches. One of Thing's most interesting insights is his description of the 'social construction of communism as a rational world view with a secret religious room at its heart'. At this heart was the notion of the USSR as a 'holy country'. Western communists, with CPSU assistance, constructed a fantasy Soviet Union for themselves, onto which they projected their own hopes and desires for a better future.

The overall picture which emerges from this book is one of tensions between basically healthy indigenous revolutionary forces and an international, suspicious of all national peculiarities and increasingly subordinate to the foreign policy needs of the USSR. The tragedy for communist movements around the world was that what they imagined to be the jewel in their crown—the USSR—was in many ways their Achilles' heel.

This is a very useful book. All the contributions, including those not mentioned here, are of a high standard. Tauno Saarela and Kimmo Rentola, the editors, should be congratulated for their efforts. However, apart from the pieces by Kevin Morgan and Kevin McDermott, which were written in English, the book would have benefited considerably from a little sub-editing by a native English speaker with some knowledge of communism. Although the language is clear and grammatically correct, it still reads like a translation. A little more polish would have been most desirable, given the high quality of its content.

Francis King
Part-time history tutor at the University of East Anglia, a freelance translator, and SHS treasurer

Chartist portraits

Stephen Roberts and Dorothy Thompson, *Images of Chartism* (Merlin Press, London, 1998), 116pp, ISBN 0-85036-475-2, £12.95 pbk.

John K. Walton. *Chartism* (Routledge, London, 1999) 90pp., ISBN 0-415-09689-8 £6.99 pbk. (Lancaster Pamphlet Series)

Historians of popular movements are often tinged with regret at the paucity of voices from the past which have survived as testaments of the nature and involvement of their subjects. So often they just are not there to answer that 'critical' question. They are of course grateful to people like David Vincent who has laboured to bring workers' biographies to the public domain. Even so it is very hard to get at the man or woman who threw the first stone. In the late-nineteenth and twentieth centuries the camera has come to the aid of the researcher. No one will be able to write a history of the revolt in China in 1989 without acknowledging the courage of that single student who stood in front of the advancing tanks of the so-called People's Army. As early as 1888–89 the match girls and London dockers were snapped and their images have become part of our understanding of the great movements they were part of enriching our knowledge of their struggles.

When we move back another fifty years to the Chartists we have only one useful photograph: of the opening rally at the great April 10th demonstration at Kennington. Some historians have used that photograph to make informed judgements about the size of the crowd as well as getting a graphic picture of the shape of rallies with multiple platforms and some sense of the social composition of the crowd. Of course we now know that cameras can be made to lie but nevertheless photography has become a vital tool of historical research. Before 1848 we have to rely visually upon even more subjective material; drawings, sketches, etchings, portraits, and cartoons. We must make of them what we can.

Historians of Chartism are in debt to Stephen Roberts and Dorothy Thompson who have brought together a comprehensive collection of illustrative material in *Images of Chartism*. The collection has over 80 illustrations, which can repay careful study. The majority are portraits of Chartist activists. It is in the nature of such material that they should be largely the well-known and middle-class figures from the movement. They are marked by their 'responsible' poses and respectable dress though there is an amiable drawing from *Reynolds Political Instructor* of the Afro-Caribbean tailor, the 60 year old William Cuffey lacking a neck-tie. Then there is a delightful picture of Chartists on a sit-in demo at a church distinctly lacking reverence.

In some ways more interesting are the drawings of crowds and groups. They are to be treated with caution of course. One certainly wonders if the members of the 1839 Convention really looked like a meeting of London bankers! But it is important to remember that they met under considerable duress and to present themselves conservatively must have seemed a good tactic. Unfortunately this particular image appears not to be sourced so it is difficult to know the illustrator's view point. The picture from *The Illustrated London News* of the Convention of 1848 suggests a much more heterogeneous gathering though its apparently open public nature is surprising given the repressive atmosphere in that year.

The limitations of the collection do not result from the work of the authors but from what is available and has been unearthed. It is excellent to have the images in one book and it should prove a valuable tool for teachers and writers at all levels. Interrogating pictures is a great group activity: interactive, instructive *and* fun.

John Walton's survey is a welcome and excellent addition to a series of short historical pamphlets, which now runs to sixty volumes. Written in a crisp readable fashion old and new debates round Chartism are integrated into the text. The author covers most aspects of the subject. It will provide an excellent primer for sixth form and undergraduate students. It should lead students to further study. As Walton shows, interest in this massively researched topic is very much alive and well.

John Charlton

Not only sex, drugs and rock 'n roll

Geoff Andrews, Richard Cockett, Alan Hooper and Michael Williams (eds), *New Left, New Right and Beyond: Taking the sixties seriously* (Macmillan, Basingstoke, 1999) ISBN 0-333-74147-6, 224pp., £45 hbk.

This text provides an engaging and accessible exploration of the contrasting perceptions of the period from those on the right who see it as an age of 'frivolity and irresponsibility' versus the left's perception of its 'inflated rhetoric and negligible achievement'. The emphasis is on how the New Left and New Right emerged out of the 1960s and impacted on 1990s' Britain. The essays reflect a healthy mix of highly researched pieces to essays which provide a more, at times, entertaining personal reflection on the period. For the specialist: Marvin Gettleman provides a very thorough survey of the myriad of New Left movements that existed throughout this period in the US; Tom Steele explores the reception of Gramsci into British cultural politics and Geoff Andrews divides the New Left into three distinctive sub-groupings. Two other very specific pieces are Alan Hooper's exploration of the nature of modernity in the context of the 1960s and Michael Williams detailed examination of two leading historians—Eric Hobsbawm and Robert Skidelsky. For those who are not specialists in the field, the collection allows the reader to look freshly at naïve assumptions they may have had about the period at the same time as they are given nostalgic reminders of the music and novel events of the time. This diversity is reflected in the contributors ranging from, say, Richard Cockett, whose notes tell us (perhaps with an attempt at wry humour) that he was 'too young to remember the sixties', to Wendy Wheeler, who allows us to take a 1960s' trip (no pun intended) down the memory lane of Camden Town to the psychedelic bookshop Compendium, and other hippy attractions.

Wheeler's 'Stars and Moons: Desire and the Limits of Marketisation' definitely scores high in the entertainment and nostalgia category. She captures the mood and spontaneity of the time when 'everyone read *Lord of the Rings*', and love was expressed by 'tree-hugging (preferably when stoned), but also makes the point that the 1990s' 'commodification of hippiedom' can only express an 'obscure desire for that earlier moment' and 'what it signified'. She combines her entertaining account with a moving reinforcement of the fact that 'creative human souls' capability of love and relatedness—truly a child of the sixties speaking-makes them far too complex to be mere commodities.

Richard Cockett's 'The New Right and the 1960s: The Dialectics of Liberation' is also noteworthy for its ability to cover a lot of ground in a lively style as well as capturing seminal moments in the sixties: notably the bizarre Jagger interview with the Archbishop of Canterbury and an analysis of some of his song lyrics, along with further commentary on some of the Beatles' songs. This combined with one or two catchy quotes from Margaret Thatcher's memoirs makes the essay all the more engaging. His trawl of key political biographies is very funny in places showing how totally out of touch with the 'swinging sixties' these people were. He argues that they would like to have reverted to 'the 1950s nirvana of monogamy and hot cocoa'. His main purpose is to debunk the populist myth of the sixties age of 'Woodstock, Carnaby Street and the Beatles' illustrating in particular the lack of substance in the supposed radicalism of the time, as well as providing a fairly thorough survey of the emergence of the New Right.

The texts of Peter Saunders, and Hilary Wainwright, politically poles apart, make interesting reading placed next to each other. However, both would have been more usefully situated near the start of the book, for they provide the clearest definitions of the New Left and New Right for non-specialist readers. Herein lies their soul similarity. Saunders expresses a *frightening* attitude to state welfare, arguing that it leads to the disintegration of social cohesion. His logic is so simple one might almost be drawn in, as he laments the demise of the Friendly Societies and the way in which communities looked out for one another before the ready hand-outs of the Welfare State. One has only to read about the many shocking cases doctors encountered when the National Health Service was first made available, home-made remedies probably doled out by a supportive if impoverished community, to see the weakness and callousness of his argument. It is a case of solidarity in adversity I would argue. Hilary Wainwright, on the other hand, shows the evolution and problems encountered post '68 for all proponents of the New Left as one, who clearly lived through these fears and concerns at firsthand—a convincing and informative account.

The final three chapters explore the way that ideas developed in the 1960s have proved to be too simplistic and idealistic. Tariq Madood, Anne Showstack Sassoon and Paul Hirst look at racial inequality, the women's movement and economic management respectively, each showing that society today is a far more complex structure than it was (or was perceived to be) in the 1960s.

Madood shows how the creation of a 'Black' identity in the 1960s, while initially helping to unite those non-white groups suffering from prejudice, failed to take into account the self identity of the different ethnic groups involved. He correctly asserts that although Afro-Caribbeans saw themselves in terms of blackness, South Asian groups were more inclined to identify themselves via their social background and/or religion. As a result, Madood argues, the response to racism cannot be limited to a set of supposed criteria (e.g. Blackness) but must take on a diverse set of cultural values and aspirations. What is more, they are values and aspirations within a British context. As Madood concludes: 'The idea, as mistakenly once supposed by Salman Rushdie, that Britain is 'Two Worlds' of black and white, has given way to a more sensitive awareness of plurality. But it is a plurality that aspires to be not just 'in' Britain but 'of' Britain.'

Despite the clearly different areas of discussion covered by Anne Showstack Sassoon and Paul Hirst, both seem to call for the need to be more flexible in thinking and our approach to society. Showstack Sassoon argues that our understanding of the past needs to be located within its own time period rather than from a retrospective position. Thus criticism of 1960s' political decisions (e.g. housing policies) should be tempered with an historical understanding of why the policy, for example, to build high-rise flats was made. Only by understanding the historical background to political policy making can we properly assess the mistakes (and triumphs) of the past. Finally, Hirst points out that changes in the structural organisation of modern society leave the dominant economic theories developed in the sixties—the left's belief in a state-controlled economy and the right's belief in a free-market economy—obsolete. Hirst argues that we need to rethink our approach adopting a more flexible, public, and piece-meal approach.

All in all, the volume is informative, accessible and entertaining. The only criticisms I would make are that I would have liked the introduction to have provided a more matter-of-fact account of what is understood by the New Left and New Right, as a route in for non-specialists. I should also have liked more of the contributors to be a little more angry at New Labour policies, but then this last point is just a personal feeling, with which, presumably, few of the contributors would agree.

Stephen Brindle teaches social studies at the University of Luton

Cutlasses and Earrings

Jo Stanley (ed.), *Bold in her Breeches: Women pirates across the ages* (Pandora Press, London, 1996) pp.xvii + 283pp., ISBN 0-04440-970-2, £7.99 pbk.

Although the title of this book focuses on women pirates, Stanley's real aim here is to highlight the invisible women who have been involved in a seafaring life. Invisible, because they have not usually featured in formal histories of seafaring. She found, for example, sailors boasting about being born at sea and yet no mention was made of any women aboard the ship. Stanley presents an interesting account of what life at sea might have been like for the women who chose or were forced to pursue it. The book grew from a personal quest to find information on a seafaring aunt about whom little was known.

The book's chapters cover both the fact and the fiction of women pirates, from being working women with seemingly little option other than seafaring or prostitution, to figures of men's fantasy. The lives of seven of the women pirates whose stories exist in history books are covered: Artemisia, Alfhuild, Grace O'Malley, Ann Bonny, Mary Reid, and Cheng I Sao. Their existence suggests, Stanley argues, that evidence of many more women who were sailors of all kinds has been suppressed or lost. But more than those actually at sea, there must have been a whole female network surrounding the sea and dockside. Those women who were deeply involved in this world as lovers, wives, mothers, sex-industry workers, informants, fences, suppliers, nurses, cooks and seamstresses are also not given a place in history. This book aims not merely to add a few women to the stories but rather to re-order the whole picture of men *en masse* working on the move.

The history of pirates in general is first examined: who they were and where they came from. Also the relationship pirates, privateers and buccaneers had with different governments, cargo and trade routes are looked at. Obviously what was heroic discovery and trade to one was piracy to another. Stanley then tries to place women into this world. There has to be some supposition about the stories involved as there is little evidence about women at sea, and much of the information that exists is anecdotal. So even though the author has to talk of women who probably were there rather than factually were, she presents a strong case. Stanley's greatest achievement is in making the reader clearly see the roles women would have played in this world, and the injustice of women not receiving their rightful place in the accounts before.

She looks briefly at women's expected roles and positions in the heyday of piracy, the 1600s and 1700s. This enables the reader to fully understand the forces that drove women—either through there being no other way of making a living, following lovers, or a desire for adventure—to the sea and possibly piracy. It may have been these expected roles that led to women's disappearance from, or poetic licence in, history books. Women's role dictated they were not at sea, indeed they were thought to be unlucky on board ships, and so they were left out of descriptions of sea life. They may also have been seen as supporting the male pirates and therefore their actions were given auxiliary rather than genuine status.

The breeches in the title indicates another example of women transcending their passive role. There is evidence to suggest many women cross-dressed as men in order to undertake jobs for which they would have been considered unsuitable. This included fighting in wars, and sailing on all sorts of ships. There are some questions about whether those who worked with a cross-dressed woman knew her to be such, as unfortunately again information about this is scarce.

After recounting some of the facts about pirates, both men and women, Stanley goes on to consider the fiction. She shows the similarities between the myths that have grown up around these factual characters and those of stories of warrior women such as *femme fatales* in literature and reports of women criminals. These similarities are also found in modern characterisations of wild women. Some examples used are of the leather-clad Mrs Peal from the cult series 'The Avengers', the characters of the feature film 'Thelma and Louise', or the idea of Mrs Thatcher wielding a cutlass. The perennial attraction of these myths may be that they appeal to both men and women. For men, they are creatures of heightened sexuality and therefore sexual appeal. To women, they break the stereotype of home-based, passive, submissive figures and instead embody adventure, challenge, and excitement.

Two of the most famous women pirates were Ann Bonny and Mary Reid who sailed on the same ship in the early eighteenth century. The fiction of these two women grew up very quickly. Much of the facts about them can be gleaned from the transcripts about their trail. Yet much of what is quoted comes not from this source but from a book, which appeared four years later in 1724.[1] Here the women were given virtuous reasons for their crimes in the style of Robin Hood. They were given explanations for the violence they showed such as in protecting a lover. Their situations were also resolved in line with the femme fatale myth, one dying in prison and one giving up the pirate's life to settle down with her husband.

Stanley has written a book that will not only appeal to pirate historians. As she draws a wider picture around these colourful characters, it would also be relevant to those interested in naval history, gender studies, and women's history.

1. Johnson, Captain Charles (1724), *A General History of the Robberies and Murders of the Most Notorious Pyrates*, published as *Daniel Defoe, A General History of the Pyrates*, Manuel Schonhorn (ed.), Dent, 1972.

Jane Tinkler

Organising the poor

John Charlton, *'It Went Just Like Tinder': The mass movement and New Unionism in Britain 1889* (London, Redwords, 1999) pp.144, ISBN 1-872208-11-8, £6.99 pbk

The Bryant and May match girls' strike of July, 1888, has long been one of the labour movement's most powerful symbols. The girls were mostly in their early teens, many suffered from 'phossy-jaw' (a disease brought on by the phosphorous they worked with) and their working conditions were atrocious. The impetus for this unprecedented strike, however, came from the actions of Annie Besant, a woman who occupied a much more comfortable social position, who was also a socialist. Annie agreed to go to the notorious Bryant and May factory in Bromley by Bow, to interview the young women for a report in her paper, *The Link*. When three girls were sacked for having spoken to Annie, 200 hundred marched out of the factory to her offices in Fleet Street, seeking her help. The match girls' strike lasted for only three weeks, but it won the right to organise a trade union. It broke the mould of exclusive craft unionism and established a new pattern of struggle, a pattern in which socialists played a key role in organising unskilled workers.

This pattern of action was repeated throughout the following summer and beyond: it became known as New Unionism. The next group of workers who took up the fight was the Beckton Gas Workers. At a public meeting in Canning Town, socialist Will Thorne launched the National Union of Gas Workers and General Labourers, focusing on the demand for an eight-hour day. Within two weeks, 3,000 had joined the union. The growing confidence among the poor of the East End exploded decisively in August 1889, when the Great Dock Strike erupted. To understand the significance of the Dock Strike, two factors must be born in mind. First, the port of London was the hub of the world's most powerful trading empire, yet, second, the 150,000 workers employed along the riverside were considered to be the most downtrodden of all. Their basic pay had remained at 5d an hour for two decades and in addition, only 10 percent of the dock workers had permanent employment. The rest were casual, competing every day to get their 'ticket' to work. Charlton quotes Ben Tillett's evocative description of this desperate struggle for survival: 'Coats, flesh, and even ears were torn off… The strong literally threw themselves over the heads of their fellows and battled through the kicking, punching, cursing crowds to the rails of the 'cage' which held them like rats—mad human rats who saw food in the ticket'.

However, when a small dispute broke out on a ship, the *Lady Armstrong*, the activist Ben Tillett seized his moment to build these ragged men into a working class. He called in socialists Tom Mann and John Burns to help launch a strike that grew rapidly peaking with 60,000 out. The strike depended on picketing, 16,000 pickets were organised, and solidarity from other workers, from as far afield as Australia and regular demonstrations which boosted strike funds and moral. The great socialist William Morris described the strike: 'this is revolt against oppression: a protest against the brute force which keeps a huge population down in the depths of the most dire degradation, for the benefit of a knot of profit-hunters…this is a strike of the poor against the rich'.

The dockers' success in establishing a union changed the face of trade unionism in London and across Britain. Out of that hot summer of struggles, which saw 'dozens of other stoppages flaring up like tinder', other lasting organisations were built. The dockers' union became the Transport and General Workers' Union and Will Thorne and Eleanor Marx set up what was to become the General and Municipal Workers' Union, with a women's branch. Old moribund unions, especially in engineering and mining were transformed by the radicalisation while for the first time shop, factory and transport workers established their own unions.

John Charlton's book is a celebration of an inspiring mass movement, but it is much more: it is also an analysis of the origins of the movement and its contradictory legacy.

As Charlton points out, despite appearances, the movement did not actually spring completely out of the blue. Prior to the strikes there had been mass mobilisations against state repression and unemployment, such as the demonstration which became known as Bloody Sunday, 1887 and a growing sense of radicalisation amongst the unskilled. Charlton places great emphasis on the Irish origins of the workers who fought back, suggesting that while the 'spirit of the Irish may have been the key factor in launching the mass movement…paradoxically, it may well have been its Irishness, its relationship to Catholic authority which proved its downfall'. There were many Irish immigrants in the East End, and New Unionism was preceded by large campaigns in solidarity with the Irish. However, there were many other groups of immigrants and indigenous English workers involved in New Unionism. The downfall of the movement had its roots in the immaturity of the movement and the weakness of the incredibly influential socialist movement at the time rather than any subservience to Catholicism.

During the years before New Unionism there had been a growing interest in Marxist and socialist publications and organisations. The main socialist organisations of the time, the Social Democratic Federation and the Socialist

League were wracked by squabbles and sectarianism, and never became mass parties, yet they also involved some of the great figures of the British socialist movement, such as Eleanor Marx, William Morris and John Lincoln Mahon. Charlton points out how this generation of socialists was at home on the streets campaigning for free speech and agitating for the eight-hour day and won an influence far beyond their size. Every strike leader was influenced by one or another socialist organisation and Marxist politics helped to strengthen the New Unionism and reinforce its orientation on women, immigrant workers and the unskilled.

Yet within a few years many of the great leaders of the 1880s had abandoned rank-and-file militancy in favour of parliamentary positions, and some, such as John Burns actually became Liberal rather than Labour sympathisers. Only Tom Mann found his way into the Communist Party when it was established in 1920. Charlton demonstrates that this was partly a reflection of the immaturity of the movement itself. The great dock strike, for example, which involved the activity of thousands of strikers, was actually ended by a committee chaired by Cardinal Manning behind the dockers' backs. The movement's leaders were necessarily inexperienced (the last mass strike had taken place in 1842) and the socialists had no consistent strategy towards the trade-union movement: some individual members played heroic roles, while others argued that strikes were an unnecessary diversion from more serious issues. This meant that the goals of the movement never matched its power and the initiative was seized by elements outside the working class who sought to contain the strikes. This in turn meant the movement was disarmed in the face of the inevitable employers' offensive. It was the success of this offensive, the defeat of strikes such as that at the Manningham Mills in 1893, that provided the impulse for an influential layer of militants to turn away from the industrial struggle in favour of winning positions in parliament to effect change on behalf of the rank and file. As Charlton points out, 'The long road to Ramsay MacDonald, Neil Kinnock and Tony Blair had begun.'

'It Went Just Like Tinder' is an important, stimulating, provocative contribution to the debates around New Unionism. It deserves to be widely read not just as a examination of events long passed but a pointer to the impact socialists can have on movements which break out unexpectedly in the future.

Judy Cox

Conspiracy on a world stage

Peter Gowan, *The Global Gamble: Washington's Faustian bid for world dominance* (Verso, London, 1999), 280pp., ISBN 1-85984-271-2, £13.00 pbk.

Peter Gowan's new book makes the audacious and compelling claim that 'globalisation' far from being what it is usually thought of, as the vast impersonal economic and technological forces behind the spread of global capitalism which evolve organically and spontaneously and to which all states to a lesser or greater degree succumb, but rather as America's Faustian 'global project', or 'global gamble' for world domination and control. Gowan argues that the central nervous system of globalisation is the present international monetary and financial regime, which he terms the Dollar-Wall Street Regime (DWSR), constructed largely by the US government out of the ashes of the Bretton Woods system in 1971 when the Nixon administration moved the dollar off the gold standard. The end of the Bretton Woods regime also meant the end of the old systems 'financial repression' designed by Keynes and Dexter White to privilege international economic development and stability over rentiers and speculators. America abolished its capital controls and the rest of the world were effectively forced to follow suit because of the dollar's superior strength, and the decisive competitive advantage enjoyed by Wall Street as by far the largest stock market and credit institution. Thereafter, the pure dollar standard and unrestricted private international financial transactions has enabled successive US administrations and business élites to exercise enormous political power to determine the internal and external political, social and economic environments of the global system of states. The transformation of domestic environments is known as neo-liberalism with the introduction of free-market capitalism and the subordination of productive sectors to financial sectors, and the consequent impetus to shift wealth, power and security away from the bulk of the working population and concentrate it in the hands of a small business élite. The transformation of the external environment of states is the force known as globalisation. This involves the opening of a state's political economy to products, companies and financial flows and operators from the core countries, making state policy dependent on decisions taken in Washington, New York and the other Atlantic capitalist powers. Neo-liberalism and globalisation then serve to reciprocally reinforce each other. The global gamble ensures that state leaderships will want what American political and business élites want, while the former retain full responsibility for the social and economic costs that befall their populations. The benefits of the global transnational order accrue to America while the disbenefits can be distributed abroad. Countries hardest hit by the DWSR include the South, and East Central and Eastern Europe. Historically, the world was moving towards globalisation and neo-liberalism well before the collapse of the Soviet bloc. However, the collapse of communism in the Soviet bloc presented American political and business élites with a diabolic temptation, reminiscent of Faust's, to make a bid for hitherto undreamed of cosmopolitan power using their combined dominance of the international monetary and financial regime and post-Cold War global military ascendancy. Therefore, successive US governments have sought to radicalise and generalise the aforementioned trends to anchor the newly emerging post-communist states, and other political economies, to American political and economic interests.

The first part of the book deals with the economics of globalisation. The main thrust of Gowan's thesis is extremely persuasive and difficult to argue with unless one is a specialist in international economics. However, there are a number of general points on individual rights and welfare with which to take issue. As an example, Gowan attempts to evaluate the American-led military campaign against Iraq during the Gulf War against the yardstick of rights-based liberalism, in terms of which America tried to justify its stance. America presented the conflict with Iraq as one between liberal justice and political oppression. However, according to Gowan America's actions were in fact entirely consistent with Groatian state rights theory which treats all states as having an equal right to exist as sovereign entities and be defended, and is at least agnostic as to the question of individual rights and welfare. Therefore, he argues that America was only concerned with restoring Kuwait's national sovereignty to the oppressive anti-democratic al-Sabah regime, and securing its vitally important oil interests. It was not interested in negotiating with Iraq because that would have handed Iraq a propaganda victory in championing Palestinian self-determination. Also, America deliberately ruled out arming a Kuwaiti popular resistance to the invasion because ultimately it would have threatened the al-Sabah regime, so supportive of US oil interests, with an anti-American democratic rebellion. America's whole strategy in the Arab World is to maintain the existing compliant unpopular regimes, like Saudi Arabia, which allow the domination of US financial and business interests. However, even if one accepts Gowan's analysis, I would argue that it grossly underrates the extent to which the military action taken against Iraq was supported by many other countries in the UN. Before the outbreak of the war Iraq failed to comply with any of the resolutions passed by the UN including a full and unconditional withdrawal. Although the military action taken by the American-led coalition lacked the express authority of the UN, it had the authoritative backing of the resolutions passed. After all, there was no UN resolution condemning US actions. I also feel that Gowan has failed to provide a convincing alternative to Desert Storm. Iraq's offer to 'negotiate' over its withdrawal from Kuwait was rejected by the Americans and other countries because Iraq failed to prove its words by deeds. The alternative idea of a Kuwaiti popular resistance to the Iraqi occupation backed by Western moral and material aid seems highly implausible. Gowan provides no detailed explanation of how this might have been practically possible, that is, how the Americans and the other western powers could have armed and trained the existing popular resistance under conditions of occupation, against the Iraqi Army which was then by far the largest in the Arab World. Therefore, I feel that Gowan's thesis of American political domination and control of the world, for all its sophistication, does not always stand up to scrutiny when looking at the detail of international political and economic issues.

A.C. Weaver

SUBSCRIBE TO SOCIALIST HISTORY

Annual subscription for individuals is
(UK) £15.00, and (Rest of World) £20.00.

Institutional and library subscription is £25 per annum.
Send requests to:

> Subscriptions,
> Rivers Oram Press,
> 144 Hemingford Road,
> London N1 1DE
> UK